NEURODESIGN

NEURODESIGN

■ ■ ■

The Art and Science of Harmonious Living

By Dr. Rachel Lynn Melvald
Psychitecture Inc.

Copyright © 2025 by Dr. Rachel Lynn Melvald

www.psychitecture.com
www.neurodesign.com

All rights reserved. This book or any portion thereof may not be reproduced or used in any manner whatsoever without the express written permission of the publisher except for the use of brief quotations in articles and book reviews.

NO AI TRAINING: Without in any way limiting the author's [and publisher's] exclusive rights under copyright, any use of this publication to "train" generative artificial intelligence (AI) technologies to generate text is expressly prohibited. The author reserves all rights to license uses of this work for generative AI training and development of machine learning language models.

Disclaimer: Portions of this book were generated by or written with the assistance of artificial intelligence technologies.

Author photograph by Amanda Friedman
Cover art and design by Richard Harrington

First Printing, 2025

ISBN-13: 978-1-962984-98-0 print edition
ISBN-13: 978-1-962984-99-7 ebook edition

Waterside Productions
2055 Oxford Ave
Cardiff, CA 92007
www.waterside.com

I should say: the house shelters day-dreaming,
the house protects the dreamer, the house allows one to dream
in peace.
—Gaston Bachelard, *The Poetics of Space*

Table of Contents

Introduction: What Is Neurodesign?	ix
PART I: The Science Behind the Art: The Origins of Neurodesign	**1**
Chapter 1: From Chaos to Harmony	3
Chapter 2: A New Norm for Living Spaces	32
Chapter 3: The Harmonious Home: Emotional, Physical, and Spiritual Well-Being	37
PART II: What Psychology Teaches Us About Harmonious Living	**69**
Chapter 4: Home as a Mirror of Self	71
Chapter 5: Foundational Psychological Models of Neurodesign	76
Chapter 6: What is Harmonious Living? The Relationship Factor	89
PART III: Neurodesign Elements for Harmonious Living	**123**
Chapter 7: Biophilia, Ergonomics, Proxemics, and Spaces of Refuge	129
Chapter 8: Our Spaces and Our Senses	139
Chapter 9: Orientation, Organization, and Personalization	152
Chapter 10: Flexibility and Beauty	164
Conclusion	171
Acknowledgments	173
Appendix A: Neurodesign Principles Through the Lens of Maslow's Hierarchy of Needs	175
Appendix B: Harmonious Home Checklist and Toolkit	183
References	191
About the Author	207
Notes	209

Introduction: What Is Neurodesign?

Let me start by answering the question: What is neurodesign? Simply stated, neurodesign is the art and science of living intentionally in our spaces and with each other. It is the connection between neurological health and interior design, and it is rooted in both ancient wisdom and modern brain science. Interior spaces have a direct impact on sensory perception, mood, cognitive function, our relationships, and overall neurological health. So by integrating insights from neuroscience, this comprehensive book will guide you in transforming your interior environments to significantly improve your mental, emotional, and physical well-being.

Neurodesign and my business, Psychitecture Inc. Design for the Mind, were founded as a philosophy, science, and methodology based on research in the fields of neuroscience, psychology, sociology, anthropology, architecture, and design. You could say I became interested and began my neurodesign research very early. As a child, starting around age six, I became obsessed with dollhouses and building blocks. Coming from a "broken home," I constantly tried to create my own sense of home. In college, I pursued dual majors in psychology and fine arts because I was interested in both. And later, I made the decision to study architecture at the highly esteemed Southern California Institute of Architecture (SCI-Arc).

As I navigated the intensely competitive studio work required for my architecture degree, my private psychotherapy practice was

Rachel Lynn Melvald

growing and demanding the same level of commitment. I was specializing more in couples therapy, and couples were coming to me in crisis mode relating to their living situations—a potential move-in together, a remodel, or a separation. Many of these couples were experiencing life transitions, and the stressors were challenging their stability. Could they make the jump to buy the home together? Could they survive their remodel? How could they separate their home in harmony? For couples buying real estate, the stakes were financially and emotionally high, often exacerbating existing wounds and requiring urgent intervention. If you've ever embarked on a design project, whether it be selecting a new sofa or doing a massive renovation, you know how stressful, confusing, and mentally exhausting the experience can be. And if you are a couple moving into a new home, this phase of life can be overwhelming since it requires each person to give up a certain degree of autonomy and often exposes their preexisting issues.

Neurodesign, the art and science of how we live intentionally in our spaces and with each other, became a methodology for intervention, growth, and transformation with which I could rescue a design project on the brink of failure. It was proving to be a niche practice that further transformed and revealed an individual's authentic self while creating an environment that reflected this transformation. My expertise in psychology and design provided the knowledge base that helped heal my clients and their relationships, enabling them to live more authentic lives through environments that supported their healing. Fundamentally, our psyche and projected environments mirror one another: Our exterior environment is a mere reflection of our interior life.

We've all heard horror stories about how a remodel nearly tore a couple apart or how a family experienced conflict because their living space didn't serve every person's needs. The COVID-19 lockdown, and the subsequent popularity of working at home, showed us how critical it is to create a living space that serves the needs of all occupants, whether romantic partners or families.

While most good designers and architects work with their clients' intentions in mind, this book demonstrates how neurodesign takes the process a step further and works with the deeper psychological needs that arise when people live together—from differing needs for work, school, leisure, self-care, and sleep to general tension or stress. My unique set of tools helps homeowners determine factors in the physical world that help them connect with a sense of wellness. I use these factors in the design process to help people recognize how their exterior environments reflect their interior lives.

Why Is This Book Important Now?
Neurodesign is especially relevant since the global pandemic forced us to live and work in new ways while allowing us the opportunity to evaluate how our exteriors and interiors elevate us or confine us. We increasingly see our living environment as a reflection of who we are and of our highest selves. By utilizing neurodesign, residents can design their work-living spaces to promote productivity while creating boundaries and space for relaxation and connection.

Every Home Tells a Story: Inspiring Stories of Transformational Spaces for Harmonized Living
The book presents a step-by-step approach to applying design tools and psychological principles to create intentional, mindful, and purposeful places of higher well-being, including case studies showcasing people who have redesigned their living situations to work better for their lives. Each story illustrates how we can create homes that are portals to our inner world and how living harmoniously can unleash the power of transformation in ourselves, our relationships, and our environment.

Keys to Your Dream Home: Design Elements for Harmonious Living

In today's rapidly changing world that can seem out of control, what we can control is our home environment. The design of our homes plays a crucial role in fostering emotional well-being, personal growth, and a deep sense of connection. A harmonious home is not simply about aesthetics or functionality; it is about creating an environment that supports the full spectrum of human experience—physical, emotional, and psychological. Homes are more than places where we sleep or eat; they are spaces where we live, grow, heal, play, create, exercise, and form meaningful connections. As we spend more time in our homes, the design of these spaces has come to the forefront as an essential component of mental health and personal well-being.

In each of the subsequent chapters, we will more deeply explore the most essential neurodesign principles that are employed in creating a harmonious home. Each design principle addresses physical comfort and functionality and speaks to deeper human needs, such as the desire for connection, emotional regulation, and self-expression. Whether it is using color psychology to evoke positive emotions, implementing flexible and adaptable spaces to support different moods, adding plants, natural light, and water features to create a calming environment, exploring how ergonomics and thoughtful furniture selection promote comfort and productivity, or integrating art and beauty to inspire awe and connection, implementing these principles demonstrates how thoughtfully designed spaces can transform how we live. Ultimately, this exploration will guide the creation of a more comfortable and functional home that nurtures the mind, body, and spirit and supports a more harmonious and fulfilling life.

Below are the significant neurodesign principles that will be employed to create a harmonious home:

1. **Biophilic Design:** Bring nature indoors by incorporating elements like indoor plants, natural materials (wood, stone), and water features. Biophilic design has been shown to reduce stress, improve cognitive function, and enhance overall well-being.
2. **Ergonomics:** Create a comfortable and functional living space by considering ergonomic principles. Choose furniture that supports good posture and comfort. Pay attention to proper lighting, adjustable workstations, and efficient organization to minimize strain and promote productivity.
3. **Proxemics:** Address how we position ourselves between others and space. In our homes, our relationships require varying degrees of closeness, intimacy, boundaries, and separation to promote healthy relationship functioning.
4. **Space of Prospect and Refuge:** Select spaces or rooms that appeal to our need to feel safe, secure, open, or hidden. The theory of "prospect and refuge" seeks to describe why certain environments feel secure and therefore meet basic human psychological needs. Environments that meet such needs allow people to observe (prospect) without being seen (refuge).
5. **Color Psychology:** Choose colors that evoke positive emotions and create a desired atmosphere. Cool colors like blues and greens can promote relaxation, while warm colors like yellows and oranges can energize and stimulate. Consider the purpose of each room when selecting colors.
6. **Lighting:** Incorporate ample natural light into your home as exposure to natural light helps regulate the circadian rhythm, promotes better sleep, boosts mood, and enhances cognitive function. Use skylights, large windows, and light-colored curtains or blinds to maximize daylight. For relaxation and sleep, use blackout shades for those sensitive to light to promote deeper REM sleep. Implementing UV light can have further stimulatory benefits that improve mood.

7. **Sensory Integration:** Incorporate a variety of sensory experiences in your home. Use textures, scents, and ambient sounds to create a multisensory environment. For example, soft textures like plush rugs, scented candles, and calming music can create a soothing ambiance.
8. **Sound:** Minimize noise pollution within your home. Excessive noise can increase stress levels and impair cognitive function. Use sound-absorbing materials like carpets, rugs, curtains, and acoustic panels to dampen sound. Consider double-glazed windows for better sound insulation.
9. **Texture:** Materials used in the home, such as marble floors versus soft rugs, affect how we feel in our home environments. Intentionally incorporating specific textures to support well-being can be seen in the design philosophy of "hygge," which incorporates warmth in materials, blankets, and pillows, fostering connection and feelings of belonging.
10. **Orientation:** Optimize views of nature from within your home wherever possible. Exposure to natural scenes, such as greenery or water, has a calming effect on the mind and can improve attention and well-being. Position seating areas near windows to take advantage of pleasant views. Watching trees sway in the wind can have a regulatory impact, shifting our emotional activation levels from activated to calm.
11. **Wayfinding:** Use signage or color to aid in spatial orientation, allowing for easier navigation of one's home in terms of direction and purpose. Wayfinding can be applied to separating rooms by color and function, as well as SMART technology to orient through vocal commands and regulate systems such as the HVAC, lighting, and alarms to help us better navigate in our living space. This is about meeting human needs.
12. **Organization:** Keep your living space organized and clutter-free. Excessive clutter can lead to stress and anxiety. Implement

effective storage solutions and regularly declutter to maintain a clean and calming environment. Consider the attachment to items that inspire and bring joy and connection versus the extreme of hoarding to hide and avoid.

13. **Personalization—Memory, Intention, Symbolism, and Meaning:** Create a space that reflects your personality and preferences. Surround yourself with meaningful objects and artwork that evoke positive emotions. Personalization fosters a sense of ownership, connection, and comfort. Family heirlooms can support or detract from a positive connection to a lineage. Homes and objects elicit emotion from our past, and how we apply this in our current space can provide a source of comfort or produce a trauma reaction.

14. **Flexible and Adaptable Spaces:** Design spaces that can be easily adapted to different activities. Having flexible spaces allows for greater versatility and accommodates various needs and moods. Consider movable furniture, room dividers, or customizable open floor plans. Boundaries like a window can serve to either support identity and individuality when closed or increase connection and intimacy when opened.

15. **Inspiring Spaces of Awe:** Populate your spaces and find real estate that allows you to feel a sense of awe, like the feeling you get when you walk into a cathedral. Take steps to emulate this sensation as you walk into your entryway. Instilling awe is not restricted to the largeness of space—you can use any of your home resources to evoke this feeling.

16. **Art and Beauty:** Implement art, such as paintings, special photos, and treasured objects, to express yourself while connecting to the greater collective. Through art, we connect to a deeper psychology of our intimate lives and to inspirational and relatable stories, images, symbols, and themes that transform us emotionally and spiritually.

The chambers of the nautilus shell embody a sense of home with a primordial design that has sheltered mollusks for more than 450 million years. The origins of neurodesign can be found in the meaningful transformation within this natural environment.

PART I
The Science Behind the Art: The Origins of Neurodesign

I developed my unique set of trauma-informed intervention tools to help distressed couples and families improve their relationships in any phase of design—from building or finding a new home to upgrading their current environment. My goal is to determine what elements in the physical world connect them to a sense of well-being and incorporate those elements into the design process. Using my neurodesign analysis method, I guide families through challenging times by combining one-on-one counseling with practical design solutions. A grounded intervention is key to my process. I work closely on-site with clients and their vendors, such as contractors and realtors, to curate homes and environments that promote healing and reflect authenticity and well-being. My approach takes into account all the needs of a home's inhabitants, whether that means creating space that supports achievement and action, establishing areas for relaxation and connection, or other solutions.

My assessment and analysis are informed by research findings of major principles born out of neuroscience, psychology, and design. They include the 14 neurodesign principles outlined in the introduction as well as these major models, which we will address in more detail in Part II.

- IMMUNOLOGY: the effect of stress on well-being and health.
- NEUROSCIENCE: how memory and place are intertwined.
- EVOLUTIONARY PSYCHOLOGY: primitive forms of defense and protection.
- MASLOW'S HIERARCHY OF NEEDS: a theory that categorizes human needs into five levels, from basic physical needs to self-actualization, with each level supporting the next.
- SENSORY PSYCHOLOGY: the study of how the senses process environmental stimuli, shaping perception and behavior.
- SOMATIC MODELS: therapies focusing on bodily awareness to help process emotions and trauma.
- DEVELOPMENTAL MODELS: Erikson's theory of eight stages of development, each with a core psychological conflict essential to personal growth.
- ATTACHMENT MODELS: models describing how early bonds with caregivers shape attachment styles that affect future relationships.
- RELATIONSHIP MODELS: Imago therapy focuses on healing relationship patterns, and the Gottman Method is a research-based technique for improving relationship satisfaction.
- FAMILY SYSTEMS: Minuchin therapy emphasizes family roles and boundaries. Bowen theory examines emotional patterns passed down in families.
- JUNGIAN ANALYTICAL STUDIES: Jung's exploration of the unconscious mind emphasizes dreams and symbols for personal growth.
- POSITIVE PSYCHOLOGY: studying factors contributing to well-being, with an emphasis on strengths, happiness, and resilience.

1

From Chaos to Harmony

As I reflect upon and write this book, I am heartbroken to see so many of my Los Angeles friends who have lost their homes in the devastating wildfires. Some of those homes had recently undergone extensive remodels, major repairs, and design negotiations, so discovering that they had been leveled is horrific. Chaos takes on another meaning after the tragic and sudden loss of a home to a natural disaster, which can be described as upheaval in terms of safety, security, and displacement from one's secure base. (In Chapter 3, I'll illustrate the foundation of safety and security using Maslow's hierarchy of needs.)

One of the most profound ways chaos can manifest in a home is through a lack of safety, particularly when a household is vulnerable to natural disasters or crime. A home that does not provide security—physically, emotionally, or psychologically—creates an ongoing sense of unease, forcing its inhabitants to remain in a heightened state of stress. When homes are located in areas prone to hurricanes, wildfires, earthquakes, or flooding, or when they are in high-crime neighborhoods, this instability affects how residents experience and interact with their living space on a daily basis.

Natural disasters introduce sudden and severe chaos into the home environment, often displacing families or forcing them to navigate dangerous conditions. A home that is not designed to withstand these events—whether due to inadequate structural integrity, lack of preparedness, or an absence of emergency measures—places its occupants at greater risk. When a storm surge floods a house, an earthquake topples furniture, or a wildfire consumes everything in its path, the loss of control is overwhelming. The destruction or partial loss of a home can disorient occupants, leaving them scrambling to rebuild their physical environment while also dealing with the emotional toll of displacement.

Beyond the immediate impact, the lingering effects of a natural disaster create ongoing instability. Individuals forced to stay in temporary shelters, live among structural damage, or struggle with unreliable utilities face ongoing disruptions in their routines. For children, losing their familiar home environment can lead to anxiety, sleep disturbances, and academic struggles, while adults may experience heightened stress, difficulty concentrating, and emotional exhaustion. The chaos extends beyond physical damage—it undermines the psychological foundation of what a home should be: a safe and stable environment.

Similarly, homes in high-crime neighborhoods often become places of stress rather than refuge. When individuals don't feel safe in their surroundings, they may experience chronic hypervigilance, always worried about potential threats outside their doors. The sound of sirens, the presence of break-ins or violent incidents nearby, or even the lack of secure locks and lighting can create an atmosphere of fear. Families living in areas with high crime rates may avoid spending time outdoors, reinforcing social isolation and limiting their ability to connect with their community. Children who grow up in unsafe environments may develop heightened stress responses, impacting their emotional regulation and long-term well-being.

When safety is uncertain, whether due to natural forces or human threats, the home is no longer a place of peace. Instead, it becomes a site of constant unpredictability, where individuals must navigate the anxiety of potential loss, violence, or instability. This persistent state of stress contributes to emotional exhaustion, fractured relationships, and diminished overall well-being, reinforcing the idea that a poorly designed or vulnerable home environment is not just an inconvenience—it is a fundamental disruption to a person's ability to feel secure and at ease in their own space.

Below is a story of the upheaval caused by a natural disaster and how neurodesign can help pick up the pieces to restore the home and a sense of safety again.

A Phoenix Rising: The Story of Jamie and Alex
Jamie and Alex loved everything about their hillside home in Malibu, with its comfortable ambiance and stunning ocean views. It was a place where they hosted casual gatherings, planned future travels, and enjoyed everyday life together. When the flames of the Woolsey Fire started to rampage through their neighborhood, they evacuated with only a few essential items, hoping the worst would pass them by. Unfortunately, the fire decimated their property, leaving only scorched rubble. In the days that followed, they were overwhelmed with disbelief and loss. But slowly, they found a quiet determination to rebuild.

With the old house gone, they resolved to create a new space that offered more than just walls and a roof. Jamie, a therapist who was familiar with creating calming environments, suggested weaving in trauma-informed design elements to help them feel at ease in their daily routines. Alex, a landscape architect, took this opportunity to bring more nature into their home, believing that open layouts, greenery, and natural light would be sources of comfort.

Building a Vision
They partnered with an architect who specialized in neurodesign, bringing together their ideas to form a balanced design:

- **Calming Spaces:** Soft, neutral colors and large windows were chosen to lend each room a sense of lightness.
- **Biophilic Design:** Living walls of greenery, a courtyard with gentle water features, and layouts that maximize natural ventilation became key elements.
- **Personalized Touches:** Alex built a dining table using beams salvaged from their original home, blending their past with their future.
- **Practical Security:** To address lingering concerns, they opted for fire-resistant materials and added a modern sprinkler system throughout.

Healing Through Creation
Once construction started, Jamie and Alex spent many weekends exploring salvage yards for unique fixtures and reclaimed doors, finding small ways to bring history into their fresh start. They also chose plants that were both drought-tolerant and known for their resilience, planting them in new gardens around the property. Friends and family helped in a variety of ways—organizing volunteer days, dropping off meals, or just offering support over coffee. Every contribution reminded Jamie and Alex that they were part of a wider community, making a challenging process more bearable.

A New Chapter
When the house was finished, it looked different from their old craftsman, but it felt distinctly their own. Sunlight poured into the living

areas, and the soft hum of water in the courtyard fountain added a calm undercurrent to daily life. Standing in the space, Jamie and Alex acknowledged the loss of their original home but found comfort in what they had created in its place. Neighbors who stopped by said the new house felt welcoming and peaceful, reflecting the couple's resilience and their conscientious decisions at every step.

Though the Woolsey Fire had been a catalyst for significant change, Jamie and Alex discovered that rebuilding allowed them to shape a home that suited their evolving needs. They hoped their story would reassure others going through similar challenges that, even amid loss, it is possible to find renewed purpose and a sense of continuity—perhaps less dramatic than rising from the ashes, but every bit as meaningful in its steady way.

Home as Refuge
Chaos in our homes forces us to confront our living situation in extraordinarily challenging ways by spotlighting overall dysregulation in home life as represented by a lack of routine, boundaries, connection with others, sense of privacy, identity, wellness, productivity, and restoration. A home should be a place of rest, connection, and security, yet for many people, their living environment is a source of stress and chaos. When a home is poorly designed—whether due to clutter, dysfunctional layouts, overwhelming sensory input, or a lack of organization—it mirrors and amplifies the chaos of daily life. The relationship between environmental psychology and home life is often underestimated, yet it plays a crucial role in how individuals function, communicate, and feel within their spaces.

Chaos in the home often manifests as **clutter**, where disorderly objects accumulate, making spaces look and feel overwhelming. Studies have shown that cluttered environments raise cortisol levels, the hormone associated with stress. When belongings don't have designated storage or surfaces are constantly covered with miscellaneous items, it reflects and perpetuates the mental and emotional clutter of the household. Piles of paperwork on kitchen counters, laundry scattered throughout multiple rooms, or an entryway overflowing with coats and shoes create a constant state of disarray that makes it difficult to mentally or physically relax. A disorganized home can lead to a never-ending cycle of frustration as inhabitants struggle to find what they need, further reinforcing a sense of disorder.

Poor spatial planning exacerbates household chaos by creating inefficiencies in how people move and interact in their space. Kitchens designed without clear work zones make meal preparation a source of stress rather than a smooth, intuitive process. Living rooms without sufficient seating or logical furniture placement lead to disjointed social interactions. Bedrooms filled with mismatched furniture or squeezed into layouts that don't prioritize rest can disrupt sleep, further compounding stress. Dysfunctional room layouts force the occupants to navigate unnecessary obstacles, mirroring the emotional and logistical friction that's present in their daily lives.

Sensory overload is another way chaos manifests in the home. Noise pollution from multiple screens, appliances, street sounds, or competing conversations creates an environment where it is difficult to focus, connect, or relax. Harsh artificial lighting that casts a cold or flickering glow can cause agitation, while an inconsistent mix of colors, textures, and decor elements can create a visually chaotic environment. A home that lacks sensory balance can overstimulate the nervous system, leaving its residents feeling drained or on edge without fully understanding why.

Poor home design often amplifies interpersonal tension, as the physical environment shapes how individuals interact within it. A lack of clearly defined spaces for different activities can lead to ongoing conflicts, especially in homes shared by multiple people. Couples may be frustrated by the lack of separate areas for work and relaxation, leading to disputes over boundaries and space ownership. Open-concept living areas without designated quiet zones can create persistent conflict between household members with differing preferences for noise levels or social interaction. Families with children may experience daily power struggles over cluttered play areas or a lack of defined zones that support both learning and play. When a home fails to accommodate its inhabitants' individual and collective needs, the result is a perpetual undercurrent of irritation and resentment.

A chaotic home life can also reflect and perpetuate **relationship dynamics**, where unresolved tensions manifest in the space itself. A couple in conflict may have a bedroom that feels cold and uninviting, mirroring the emotional distance between them. A home filled with half-finished projects or neglected repairs can symbolize a family struggling with emotional stagnation or avoidance. Disorganization in shared areas may indicate a lack of communication regarding household responsibilities. The way a home looks and functions often reveals deeper insights into the emotional state of those who live within it.

The impact of household chaos extends beyond momentary frustrations—it contributes to chronic stress, burnout, and emotional exhaustion. When people feel overwhelmed by their living environment, they may experience decision fatigue, which can lead to avoidance behaviors or a sense of helplessness. Over time, this cycle of disorder can zap motivation, making it even harder to regain control over the space. Studies indicate that people who live in chronically disordered environments are more likely to experience anxiety and depression, as their surroundings reinforce a sense of instability and lack of control.

Sleep disruption is another direct consequence of household chaos. Bedrooms that are cluttered, noisy, or poorly lit make it difficult for individuals to unwind at the end of the day, resulting in disrupted sleep patterns. Parents trying to establish bedtime routines for children may struggle if the home lacks spaces that promote calm and relaxation. Without intentional design that supports rest, sleep quality suffers, further exacerbating stress and irritability during waking hours.

The chaos of home life became more apparent than ever during the COVID-19 pandemic lockdowns. As homes were suddenly transformed into workspaces, classrooms, and social hubs, the limitations of design became glaringly obvious. The spaces that once served as places of retreat now had to accommodate round-the-clock activity, leading to increased stress, frustration, and dysfunction. Families struggled to share space efficiently, couples faced new challenges in balancing work and personal time, and individuals found themselves overwhelmed by clutter, noise, and lack of separation between their various roles. The pandemic highlighted just how much a poorly designed home could compound stress, while those with adaptable, functional spaces fared better in managing the disruptions of lockdown life.

A Home in Chaos: An Introvert/Extrovert During COVID-19

Megan and Jake had been living together for six years, navigating their differences in personality and lifestyle. Megan was socially outgoing, and she thrived on connection, frequent meetups with friends, and the energy of public spaces. Jake, on the other hand, struggled with depression and needed solitude and time alone to recharge. Before the pandemic, their home had functioned as a flexible space—Megan spent much of her time outside of it, while Jake used it as a retreat from the outside world. This arrangement worked because they had balance—Megan found social fulfillment elsewhere, and Jake had a space where he could be alone when needed.

When the COVID-19 lockdown began, their once-functional routine collapsed. Cooped up together, the stark contrast in their needs became impossible to ignore. Megan, restless and craving interaction, felt suffocated in their apartment and was desperate for a sense of normalcy and connection. Jake, already prone to depression, felt increasingly overwhelmed by the lack of personal space and retreated further into himself. Their home, which had once provided independence and comfort, now felt like a shared cage, which intensified their underlying tensions.

The physical space, designed without clear distinctions between communal and private areas, exacerbated their struggles. Their open-concept living area, which once seemed modern and inviting, left no room for Jake to isolate when he needed silence. The lack of a dedicated workspace forced Megan to conduct virtual social interactions and work calls from the same areas where Jake sought refuge, leaving him feeling constantly exposed. Clutter began accumulating—unfinished projects, scattered belongings, and unwashed dishes—all of which added to Jake's feelings of emotional paralysis and Megan's growing frustration.

The tension became palpable. Jake withdrew further, spending hours in the bedroom with the curtains drawn, while Megan paced the small apartment, desperate for stimulation. When she tried to engage him, he shut down, needing space she couldn't provide. When he asked for quiet, she felt rejected, yearning for the lively interactions that had once been so easy to find outside their home. Their sanctuary had turned into a pressure cooker, each feeling trapped in a space that wasn't serving their emotional needs.

Realizing that their home environment was fueling their struggles, they sought help from an environmental psychologist specializing in mental health and spatial design. Through guided discussions, they identified the ways their home was contributing to their disconnect and how simple design adjustments could create boundaries that supported both their individual and shared needs.

They began by creating clear zones within their space—Megan designated a corner of the living room as her workspace and social area, allowing Jake the ability to retreat without interruption. Jake, in turn, transformed the bedroom into a true recovery space by introducing softer lighting, calming textures, and noise-canceling elements to help him recharge without feeling like he was shutting Megan out. They adjusted the layout of their shared spaces, decluttered, and used subtle design cues, like separate seating areas and adjustable lighting, to define when the home was a place of togetherness and when it was a place of solitude.

These changes didn't erase their differences, but they allowed them to navigate their home life more intentionally. Megan found new ways to stay connected without encroaching on Jake's need for isolation, and Jake felt less overwhelmed knowing he had a designated space where he could recover without guilt. Over time, their home transformed from a source of conflict into a place that supported both of their needs, allowing them to coexist more peacefully during an otherwise chaotic time.

This case study demonstrates how environmental stressors, when left unaddressed, can magnify underlying relationship tensions. Megan and Jake's struggles weren't simply about the pandemic—they were about the ways their home had become incompatible with their emotional needs. By making minor but meaningful adjustments to their space, they regained a sense of balance, proving that sometimes the key to navigating differences starts with redesigning the environment in which they unfold.

Torn Apart by Home Transitions
I often hear clients say about a home transition, "It nearly tore us apart." And I understand. Moving, a death, and then a remodel

can be considered significant stressors in life. I mean, how many remodeling horror stories have you heard? A remodel, by definition, uproots not only the structure of a home but also a relationship in terms of its values, preferences, finances, and sense of grounding. When I was working with a couple remodeling their primary bathroom, the leaky pipes seemed symbolic of an emotional leak in their relationship communication and functioning. A home remodel, often envisioned as an exciting step toward improvement, can unexpectedly strain even the most solid relationships. Behind the allure of new countertops and flawlessly painted walls lies a turbulent journey filled with unforeseen challenges that can bring buried conflicts to the surface.

The Emotional Toll of Home Transitions
Major home transitions, whether it's a move, a remodel, or even the loss of a long-time home due to external circumstances, can create emotional upheaval. People often have a strong sentimental attachment to their homes; they serve as spaces of refuge, memories, and personal identity. Disrupting that space, even in the name of progress, can be jarring.

A remodel forces the occupants to confront their personal needs, aesthetic desires, and expectations for how their home should function. While it may seem like a straightforward process—hire a contractor, pick out materials, and watch the transformation unfold—the reality is much more complicated. Decisions about color schemes and layouts quickly become symbolic of deeper relationship issues, such as conflicting values, control, and even financial priorities.

Take, for example, a couple I worked with who had vastly different design preferences. The husband, a minimalist, preferred a sleek, modern look, while the wife leaned toward warmth, vintage pieces, and eclectic textures. Each tile and paint swatch turned into a battleground, representing not just an aesthetic preference but also a statement about their identity and the compromises they had made in their marriage.

Decision Fatigue and Conflict Escalation

One of the hidden stressors of a home remodel is decision fatigue. Remodeling requires constant decision-making, from selecting flooring to choosing cabinet hardware. Each choice adds another layer of emotional weight, especially for couples already struggling with communication.

Research has shown that when individuals experience decision fatigue, they are more likely to become irritable, impatient, and prone to conflict (Baumeister et al. 1998). In home transitions, this fatigue can manifest as passive-aggressive remarks, avoidance, or full-blown arguments over seemingly minor details.

In therapy sessions, many couples report feeling that their partner "never listens" or "doesn't respect their taste," but what lies beneath is often a broader struggle for control and validation. A home, after all, is not just a physical structure—it's a shared vision of a future, and when that vision isn't aligned, the results can be explosive.

Financial Strains and the Stress of the Unknown

Another major pressure point in home transitions is finances. Remodeling budgets are notoriously difficult to stick to, with unplanned expenses emerging at every turn. This can put a financial strain on couples who have different spending habits or attitudes toward money.

A husband who prioritizes long-term investments may become frustrated when his wife insists on premium fixtures, viewing them as an unnecessary indulgence. A wife who values quality craftsmanship may feel dismissed when her husband pushes for more budget-friendly alternatives. These financial conflicts don't just pertain to the remodel—they reveal underlying dynamics about financial control, shared priorities, and trust.

One couple I worked with reached a near-breaking point over budgeting disagreements. The wife saw the remodel as her opportunity to finally build the dream kitchen she had envisioned for years, while the husband was focused on cost-cutting measures in anticipation of potential financial downturns. Their sessions revolved less around backsplash options and more around their fundamental differences in security and risk-taking.

The Need for Control in Uncertain Environments
Psychological studies suggest that humans seek control as a way to manage stress and uncertainty. A home remodel, with its delays, contractor mishaps, and unexpected expenses, can make people feel powerless. In response, individuals may try to overcompensate by micromanaging every detail, leading to friction with their partner who may not share the same approach.

For example, one spouse might obsessively monitor the remodel's progress, questioning the contractor's every move and rechecking costs. Meanwhile, their partner, overwhelmed by the constant scrutiny, may withdraw emotionally to avoid discussions about the remodel altogether. This dynamic creates resentment, with one partner feeling unheard and the other feeling burdened by relentless oversight.

Loss of Routine and Increased Stress Levels
Disruptions in routine also play a significant role in remodeling-related stress. Daily habits, from morning coffee rituals to bedtime routines, become fragmented. If a kitchen is under construction, meal prep becomes chaotic. If a bathroom is being remodeled, basic hygiene routines become inconvenient. These disruptions lead to heightened stress and impact overall well-being.

In a study conducted by the *Journal of Environmental Psychology*, researchers found that disruptions in personal spaces lead to increased anxiety and decreased cognitive function (Evans and Wener 2007). This aligns with what many clients report during a remodel: They feel "on edge" all the time, as if their home is no longer a place of rest but rather a construction zone fraught with uncertainty.

Under Construction: When Love Meets Renovation
I heard a story about a couple restoring an old Brooklyn brownstone. Their relationship imploded while the foundation cement was being poured. The couple's foundation, symbolized by the cement pour, showed how the wife wanted her husband to be more ambitious financially and stronger in how he carried the couple, and her resentment literally "poured out" when she realized he was not motivating this task. Financial strain, delayed timelines, power dynamics, and preferences in design can all challenge the status quo. A crisis can break a relationship or, if supported through it, can lead to an opportunity for incredible growth, both individually and in the relationship. The story illustrates how a crisis can become an opportunity for growth when neurodesign techniques are applied.

Stress and Decision Fatigue:
Renovations demand countless decisions, from paint colors to layout changes. When partners have differing tastes or priorities, disagreements can spiral into arguments, turning once-harmonious couples into adversaries.

Financial Strain:
Budgets often balloon beyond initial estimates, forcing difficult conversations about spending and savings. One partner may prioritize aesthetics, while the other leans toward practicality, resulting in conflicts over financial priorities.

Disrupted Routines and Privacy:
The chaos of construction—constant noise, dust, and a lack of personal space—leaves couples feeling unmoored. Losing the sanctuary of home can magnify frustrations and make small annoyances feel insurmountable.

Unrealized Expectations:
Renovations are tied to dreams of a better future, but delays, mistakes, or mismatched visions can lead to disappointment. One partner may feel their desires are being overlooked, which can sow feelings of resentment.

Communication Breakdown:
The stress of a remodel can expose weaknesses in communication. Without healthy dialogue, misunderstandings and blame can erode trust and connection.

Resolution and Growth:
A remodel can be a crucible for conflict, but it can also offer growth opportunities. With intentional communication, shared compromises, and professional guidance, couples can turn a challenging experience into a deeper bond. By focusing on their shared goals and embracing the journey together, couples can emerge stronger—with a beautiful home and a renewed sense of partnership. "Under Construction" reveals that remodeling is more than just transforming a house; it is about rebuilding relationships, one nail and one conversation at a time.

Strategies for Navigating a Home Transition
Without Relationship Breakdown
While the stress of a remodel is inevitable, there are strategies couples can use to mitigate its impact on their relationship:

1. **Set Clear Communication Boundaries**. Establish guidelines for how decisions will be made. Some couples find it helpful to divide responsibilities, with one partner handling design elements and the other managing logistics.
2. **Create a Shared Vision**. Before starting a remodel, discuss long-term goals for the home. What atmosphere do you both want to create? How does this remodel align with your lifestyle? These discussions circumvent last-minute conflicts about design choices.
3. **Establish a Realistic Budget**. Having a financial plan with contingency funds reduces stress when unexpected expenses arise. Couples should agree beforehand on what areas are worth splurging on and where they're willing to cut costs.
4. **Designate "Chaos-Free" Zones**. If possible, maintain at least one untouched area in the home where normal routines can continue. This practice helps provide a sense of stability during an otherwise disruptive period.
5. **Seek Professional Guidance**. Hire a neurodesigner!

Guidance Through a Remodel

Emily and Ryan were excited about remodeling their first home together. Emily envisioned a bright, airy space filled with modern, minimalist touches. Ryan craved rustic charm with warm, earthy tones. What began as an exciting venture soon turned into a battlefield. Each choice—paint colors, materials, and layout—became a source of conflict.

As their arguments grew frequent and intense, both felt unheard and frustrated. Exhausted and at an impasse, they realized they needed somebody to coach them through the dynamics of a remodel while supporting their differences in design needs. Ultimately, they turned to me as a neurodesigner to help them navigate their differences and design a home that would suit both their preferences and their relationship.

The Neurodesigner's Intervention

1. Understanding the Couple's Needs
I began by conducting individual interviews and then had a joint session with Emily and Ryan. I explored their aesthetic preferences, emotional triggers, and how they envisioned using each space. I also asked about their stress points during the remodeling process.

Through these discussions, I was able to identify their underlying needs: Emily desired simplicity and order to ease her anxiety, while Ryan wanted warmth and comfort to feel grounded after long workdays.

2. Bridging Preferences with Neurodesign
I introduced the couple to neurodesign principles, emphasizing how thoughtful design could balance their needs while fostering harmony in their relationship.

- **Shared Spaces:** I proposed blending Emily's modern aesthetic with Ryan's rustic charm. In the living room, for instance, I suggested sleek furniture in neutral tones paired with reclaimed wood accents and a textured area rug.
- **Personal Retreats:** Recognizing the importance of individual space, I designed a minimalist reading nook for Emily and a cozy, rustic office for Ryan. These areas would give them room to recharge independently.
- **Color Psychology:** I helped them select a color palette that combined Emily's love for soft whites with Ryan's preference for earthy tones, creating a cohesive and calming atmosphere.
- **Harmonious Flow:** I emphasized the importance of spatial flow, suggesting layouts that would naturally guide movement and reduce stress points. For example, I redesigned the kitchen to promote easy collaboration, enabling Emily and Ryan to cook together without stepping on each other's toes.

3. Coaching Communication

Beyond design, I acted as a mediator. I taught Emily and Ryan how to constructively articulate their needs and prioritize shared goals. For instance, I encouraged them to frame their disagreements as opportunities to collaborate rather than compete. I also introduced decision-making frameworks, such as "must-haves versus nice-to-haves," to help them prioritize and compromise more effectively.

4. Fostering Harmony Through Design

I integrated design elements specifically intended to nurture harmony in their relationship. I suggested they create a gallery wall of photos and mementos to celebrate their journey together. I also incorporated features like a dual-purpose dining table—ideal for hosting large gatherings or enjoying intimate dinners—to strengthen their bond through shared experiences.

The Transformation

As the remodel progressed, Emily and Ryan began to see the project as a partnership rather than a struggle. They found joy in combining their ideas.

When the remodel was complete, their home was a perfect reflection of their collaboration:

- The kitchen featured sleek cabinets paired with a natural stone backsplash, marrying modern and rustic styles.
- The open floor plan felt uncluttered yet inviting, with strategic lighting that enhanced both Emily's need for brightness and Ryan's desire for warmth.
- Their private retreats were tailored to their needs, offering solace and balance.
- Shared spaces were intentionally designed to encourage connection, like a cozy, centrally located living room and a dining area perfect for both family meals and entertaining friends.

A Home Built on Understanding
Emily and Ryan were more than happy with the finished design—they were grateful for the journey. Neurodesign guidance not only transformed their home but also strengthened their relationship. They learned to navigate challenges with empathy and teamwork and carried those skills into other aspects of their lives. For Emily and Ryan, I was more than just their neurodesigner; I was a coach, a mediator, and a bridge between their dreams, proving that thoughtful design is more than just creating beautiful spaces—it's also about cultivating connection, well-being, and harmony.

The Science to Restoring Home Harmony: An Expanded Explanation of Neurodesign
Let's dive a little deeper into the science of neurodesign. Neurodesign is a human-centered design approach that integrates insights from neuroscience and psychology to create environments tailored to its inhabitants' emotional, mental, and physical needs. It recognizes that the spaces we inhabit profoundly influence our behavior, relationships, and well-being. A neurodesigner considers how every element of a home—from layout to lighting, color to texture—can support its inhabitants' diverse needs and enhance their quality of life.

Supporting Achievement and Action
Do you sometimes feel unmotivated in your home space? What if your home office could reflect your career's momentum? A well-designed home promotes productivity and goal-oriented behavior by creating spaces that encourage focus and energy:

- **Workspaces:** For remote workers or students, neurodesign emphasizes ergonomic furniture, adjustable lighting, and calming colors that enhance focus and reduce distractions. Placing your desk near natural light or incorporating biophilic elements like plants can boost cognitive performance.

- **Activity Zones:** Open layouts in kitchens or multifunctional rooms encourage movement and collaboration, supporting active lifestyles and encouraging creativity.

Building Areas for Relaxation
Our homes are our refuge—a place to relax and restore, where we find respite from the busy outside world we cannot control. Neurodesign recognizes the importance of rest and recovery in today's fast-paced world. Relaxation spaces are crafted to provide a sanctuary from stress and include:

- **Restful Bedrooms:** Features like soft, neutral colors, blackout curtains, and noise-dampening materials help promote deep, restorative sleep.
- **Cozy Retreats:** Reading nooks or meditation corners use calming textures, gentle lighting, and comforting scents to create pockets of peace.

Facilitating Connection
Although we can find solace and peace in our homes, we know that too much isolation and not enough human connection can be harmful to our physical and mental health. A recent noteworthy publication on the health risks associated with isolation comes from the former US Surgeon General, Dr. Vivek Murthy. In May 2023, he issued an advisory titled *Our Epidemic of Loneliness and Isolation* that draws on extensive research showing how social isolation and chronic loneliness can increase the risk of serious health problems—from cardiovascular disease and depression to cognitive decline. According to the advisory, the impact of persistent isolation on overall health is comparable to smoking up to 15 cigarettes a day, underscoring the serious toll that the lack of social connection can take on both physical and mental health.

Human connection is vital for emotional health, and neurodesign incorporates areas that encourage interaction and bonding via:

- **Social Spaces:** Living and dining rooms are designed to have comfortable seating that promotes face-to-face conversations. Circular furniture layouts or shared focal points, like a fireplace, can strengthen community and togetherness.
- **Interactive Features:** Interactive elements, such as shared message boards, family activity stations, or game corners, reinforce collaboration and communication.

Harmonizing the Home Environment
Have you ever walked into a place and felt it had a good vibe? That positive vibe might even draw you back to that house or make you want to emulate it in yours. In neurodesign, we purport that there is science behind "a good vibe" and that you can create it too, given the right tools. Harmonizing an environment can be broken down into some essential neurodesign concepts. In addition to functional zoning, neurodesign ensures the home feels cohesive and emotionally supportive by:

- **Color Psychology.** Thoughtfully chosen color palettes can evoke specific moods, such as blues for calm, yellows for happiness, and greens for balance.
- **Sensory Integration.** Balancing light, sound, and tactile elements ensures the home is soothing to the senses. Soft rugs, ambient lighting, and acoustic panels reduce sensory overwhelm.
- **Flow and Balance.** Strategic layouts prevent clutter and create seamless movement between rooms, reducing stress and increasing comfort.

Rachel Lynn Melvald

The Neurodesign Difference
The neurodesign difference lies in its holistic approach to shaping living environments that go beyond mere aesthetics to address the diverse needs of those who live in them. By tailoring spaces to support productivity, relaxation, and connection, neurodesign creates homes that resonate with everyone's unique rhythms and aspirations. Productivity is enhanced through thoughtfully designed work areas that optimize focus and efficiency, integrating elements like ergonomic furniture, natural lighting, and minimal distractions. For relaxation, neurodesign crafts serene spaces that promote mental and physical recovery, using calming colors, soft textures, and sensory-friendly features.

At the same time, it prioritizes fostering connections by designing social spaces that encourage interaction and shared experiences through intentional layouts and inviting atmospheres. This comprehensive approach ensures that every corner of the home contributes to a sense of well-being, harmony, and functionality. Ultimately, neurodesign transforms a house into a nurturing sanctuary where its inhabitants can live and thrive.

Design as a Support System

> "Rachel has been called the 'Marie Kondo of Home Design' and has created a system for developing an inspiring and supportive living space while supporting the relationships between the inhabitants."
>
> —Anonymous

Earning the moniker "the Marie Kondo of Home Design" for my groundbreaking approach to transforming living spaces into havens of inspiration, connection, and support has been an honor. Unlike traditional interior designers who focus primarily on aesthetics, I integrate principles of psychology and neuroscience to create environments that look beautiful and nurture their inhabitants' emotional and relational well-being. By blending insights from neuroscience, sociology, psychology, ergonomics, color psychology, wayfinding, and cognitive science, I create holistic environments that meet the unique needs of my clients.

In addition to neurodesign techniques for saving a remodel and home, having the right support system that can guide a couple or a design project can make it or break it. Interior designers and architects often say they play therapists to their clients, but it's important to have the skill set to work effectively with them. This is where neurodesign's multifaceted approach comes into play.

Blueprint for Love: Rebuilding a Relationship with Neurodesign
Sophia and Max had always dreamed of renovating their small suburban home into a modern sanctuary. With their growing family in mind, they initiated a remodel, envisioning sleek open spaces, a light-filled kitchen, and serene bedrooms. But as the months wore on, mounting stress overshadowed their shared vision. Decisions turned into debates. Sophia wanted the kitchen island in one place; Max insisted it belonged in another. The endless choices, unexpected expenses, and disruption of their daily lives amplified every tiny disagreement. Their relationship was cracking under the pressure—just like the old plaster walls they were tearing down. Desperate to find common ground, Sophia stumbled upon an article about neurodesign. Intrigued, she suggested to Max that they approach their remodel differently—not just to create a beautiful house, but a home that nurtured their relationship.

A New Approach
With the help of a neurodesign expert, they refocused their renovation through the lens of how the spaces might affect their behavior

and emotions. Together, they prioritized design choices that would strengthen connection, reduce stress, and align with their shared values.

1. Design for Connection:
Their expert recommended reimagining the kitchen as a social hub. They placed the island centrally, ensuring it was large enough for meal prep and family gatherings. Soft, rounded edges reduced feelings of tension, and warm lighting created an inviting atmosphere.

2. Biophilic Elements for Calm:
Sophia and Max added wooden accents and a stone feature wall. Large windows and indoor plants brought the calming influence of nature into their home, soothing their minds and encouraging a sense of harmony.

3. Spaces for Individuality and Togetherness:
Recognizing the importance of personal space, they incorporated a small reading nook for Sophia and added a workshop in the garage for Max. These personal sanctuaries gave them room to recharge, while a cozy living room with comfortable seating was available when they wanted family bonding time.

4. Optimizing Flow for Ease:
A clutter-free layout became a top priority. They worked with their designer to create built-in storage and well-thought-out organization systems. The streamlined spaces reduced visual stress and cut down on arguments about messes and misplaced items.

Healing Through the Process
As the remodel progressed, so did their relationship. Intentionally designing their home became a shared project that rekindled their

partnership. Decisions were no longer about "winning" but about creating a space that served them both. They laughed as they chose paint colors together, shared their excitement as they watched the construction take shape, and celebrated small milestones—a finished floor and a painted wall. The neurodesign principles gave them a framework for understanding how their physical environment shaped their emotions, helping them be kinder and more patient.

A Home for the Future
Sophia and Max stood together in their transformed home when the remodel was complete, and they were thrilled, not only with the results but also with how they had grown as a couple. The open, airy spaces reflected their aesthetic preferences and the lessons they had learned about compromise and connection. Their kitchen was now the heart of their home, where meals were made and stories were shared. Their private spaces allowed them to be themselves, while their communal areas brought them closer. For Sophia and Max, the renovation had become more than a physical transformation; it had become a journey of growth and renewal. Their home, designed with love and intention, now symbolized the strength of their partnership and the promise of their future together.

Home as Sanctuary
Good design is good for our health, environment, and relationships. Architecture has increased in importance and popularity as we move into a time when our living environment more closely reflects who we are. We are now facing our homes and environments as if they are facing us, and they are speaking to us and saying, "We reflect your highest selves!"

The COVID-19 pandemic reshaped our relationship with our homes, as they became more than just places to eat and sleep—they transformed into multifunctional spaces where we lived, worked, studied, and sought refuge from a chaotic world. This shift highlighted a growing need for homes that are functional and supportive of mental, emotional, and physical health. During the pandemic, we had more time to scrutinize and, better yet, evaluate how our exteriors and interiors either elevated or confined us. We were faced with work in ways we hadn't experienced before, and variables such as lighting, interior space, room and design functionality, color, objet d'art, art, and furniture suddenly seemed to be saying, "What is my purpose and meaning in your life?" It was as if we were evaluating our walls while evaluating ourselves. Do we like that chair, or have we had it there for no good reason? Or is that chair a relic from our grandparents' house and holds significant meaning and connection to our lineage?

As we evaluate our space, we might assess ourselves and consider what our continued connection is to our past and lineage and what we are not making room for in our present. We consider mental health during the winter, when less sunlight can lead to seasonal affective disorder, and determine which treatments, such as light therapy, might lift our serotonin levels. We need to give the same considerations to all the elements in our living design environment. For example, your favorite color may be red, which is great for lipstick, but that doesn't always reverberate on our wall the same way; inducing rageful vibration in one can elicit passion in another.

Just as our increasing sensitivity to our living environment has promoted self-reflection and transformed parts of our environment, we can also see this in our relationships. Which phase of cohabitation we are in has its unique challenges in giving up one's autonomy to integrate with a partner in a new space. Should a commitment-phobe, or better stated, one who is insecure in their self-development, hold their man cave or she shed to preserve a space for independence? This would be a design treatment to consider. A family that doesn't want their aging parents to go into a nursing home will consider a guest house or a mother-in-law layout when designing a new home. As in our relationships and our self-development, our spaces are fluid and ever-changing.

Harmonious design supports the resilience of healthy relationships and helps all inhabitants in the home become the healthiest they can be.
Our homes are not just places we live—they are environments that profoundly influence how we feel, interact, and grow. Harmonious design facilitates a sense of balance and alignment among the people sharing a space, creating an atmosphere that nurtures healthy relationships. By addressing the needs and personalities of each inhabitant, intentional design reduces conflict, promotes understanding, and strengthens connection. When everyone in the home feels seen and supported, it becomes a space where each person can thrive, both individually and together, becoming the healthiest and most fulfilled versions of themselves.

Research shows the health benefits of intentional design
Scientific studies have consistently shown that intentional design can improve physical and mental health. For example, access to natural light regulates sleep cycles and boosts mood, while thoughtful layouts reduce stress and create functional flow. Colors influence our emotions, with calming tones reducing anxiety and vibrant hues encouraging energy and creativity. Design that incorporates biophilic elements, such as plants and natural materials, has been proven to lower cortisol levels and improve cognitive function. By leveraging these principles, intentional design transforms spaces into tools for health and well-being.

Access to natural light plays a crucial role in regulating circadian rhythms, which in turn affects sleep quality and mood. Alkozei et al. (2017) found that exposure to blue wavelength light is associated with positive mood states and sleep initiation. Similarly, Boubekri et al. (2014) showed that office workers with the greatest access to daylight had better sleep quality and overall health compared to those in artificially lit environments. This highlights the importance of incorporating ample natural light into architectural design to promote mental well-being.

Thoughtful layouts and clutter reduction have also been shown to significantly impact stress levels and cognitive function. Research by Saxbe and Repetti (2010) indicated that individuals who described their homes as cluttered or chaotic exhibited higher cortisol levels, a biomarker of stress. Cluttered spaces can create cognitive overload, making it difficult to focus and process information efficiently (McMains and Kastner 2011). Taking steps to organize your environments to minimize clutter and improve spatial flow can lead to reduced stress and greater mental clarity.

Color psychology and material choices in interior design also affect emotional states. Küller et al. (2009) found that specific colors and lighting conditions influence psychological mood, with cool tones such as blues and greens promoting relaxation, while warm colors like reds and oranges stimulate energy and alertness. Additionally, natural materials, such as wood and stone, have been linked to feelings of comfort and reduced stress (Gillis and Gatersleben 2015).

Biophilic design, which integrates natural elements into indoor spaces, has been widely studied for its positive health effects. Nieuwenhuis et al. (2014) conducted field experiments showing that workplaces filled with a plethora of plants boosted productivity by 15% and significantly enhanced employees' well-being. Similarly, Ulrich, R.S. (1984) found that hospital patients who had a view of nature recovered more quickly and required less pain medication compared to those without natural views, demonstrating the tangible health benefits of biophilic environments.

Beyond aesthetics, intentional design directly impacts health and well-being. Söderlund and Newman (2017) examined how biophilic architecture reduces stress and concluded that incorporating natural elements within built environments results in lower physiological stress responses and improved mood. These findings align with broader research indicating that exposure to natural elements in residential and commercial settings improves mental and physical health outcomes.

The convergence of these studies underscores how intentional design shapes environments to support well-being. As our understanding of environmental psychology grows, prioritizing these design principles will become increasingly essential in creating more functional living and working environments.

2

A New Norm for Living Spaces

During the pandemic, I worked with many couples challenged by the confines of their living environment. The pandemic bound us to our homes, where we had to face our walls, ourselves, and our relationships. My work in neurodesign became even more vital. Whether it was as simple as putting in a divider in a living room to separate office and home life or implementing separate lighting for mood, it had anecdotal and clinical impact.

The COVID-19 global pandemic forced an unprecedented shift in how we lived, worked, and connected, transforming our homes from places of rest and retreat into the epicenters of our lives. Dining rooms became makeshift offices, bedrooms doubled as classrooms, and living rooms became in-home gyms. This sudden need for our homes to fill every role created stress and a profound sense of disconnection. The boundaries between work and relaxation, school and family time blurred into chaos, leaving most people feeling trapped and overwhelmed. Yet, this collective experience also sparked a powerful realization: Our homes are not static structures but dynamic ecosystems that profoundly influence our mental health, relationships, and productivity. The lockdown forced us to rethink our surroundings and transform them into spaces that could adapt to the complexity of our lives, offering both function and comfort in what was a very stressful and uncertain time.

Locked Down at Home: A Pandemic Story of Change
When the pandemic hit, life as Erin and her family knew it was turned upside down. Suddenly, the house that once felt spacious and welcoming felt cramped and chaotic. Erin worked as a graphic designer, her husband, James, transitioned to remote IT work, and their two kids, Mia and Lucas, shifted to online school. So their home now had to function as an office, a classroom, a gym, and everything in between.

At first, they tried to adapt by carving out makeshift spaces—Erin claimed the dining table for her work while James set up a desk in a corner of the family room. The kids alternated between their bedrooms and the living room for online classes. But within weeks, conflicts began to emerge. The dining room was always cluttered with papers, James's work calls disrupted everyone else, and the kids complained about their inability to focus. The lack of boundaries blurred every aspect of their lives.

Erin realized something had to change when, one afternoon, she snapped at Mia for leaving her art supplies on the table—a space Erin had unofficially claimed. It wasn't about the art supplies but rather the overwhelming feeling that the house needed some serious adjustments in order to serve their needs during this forced confinement. Determined to create harmony, Erin dove into research and discovered the concept of intentional home design. Inspired by neurodesign principles, she reimagined their home to function for this new reality.

The Transformation

1. Defining Zones:
The first step was creating purpose-driven zones. Erin repurposed a small alcove near the kitchen as her workspace, and the dining table returned to its original function. James moved his desk to a corner of the spare bedroom, allowing him to close the door and minimize noise. Erin bought Mia and Lucas desks for their rooms and customized shelves and organizers for their school supplies.

2. Establishing Boundaries:
Erin set up folding screens to separate the kids' play area, while rugs and lighting were used to define Erin's workspace. The kids decorated their desks with personal items, helping them mentally shift into "school mode."

3. Enhancing Comfort and Functionality:
Because everyone was spending more time sitting, Erin invested in ergonomic chairs and better lighting. She decluttered and reduced the visual chaos that had been contributing to their stress.

4. Creating Shared and Private Spaces:
To balance togetherness and individuality, Erin set up a cozy family corner in the living room with plush seating and a bookcase for all their games and puzzles. She also made it clear that everyone's personal spaces were off-limits during work or school hours, respecting boundaries they all desperately needed.

5. Adding Nature and Comfort:
Finally, Erin brought in elements of nature—houseplants, an indoor herb garden, and a bird feeder outside the kitchen window. These small changes brought life into their home and offered moments of calm amid the uncertainty.

A New Rhythm
Over time, the changes began to have an impact. James found it easier to focus on his work without constant interruptions. The kids were more engaged in their schoolwork, and Erin finally felt she had a space that sparked creativity rather than frustration. They all loved spending evenings in the family corner where they could unwind away from their screens. The pandemic had reshaped their lives, but instead of tearing them apart, Erin's intentional approach to rethinking their home brought them closer together. Their house became a sanctuary that supported every facet of their lives. Through the challenges that the pandemic presented, Erin learned an invaluable lesson: When the world outside feels chaotic, we can create spaces inside that can provide the stability and peace we need to thrive.

What Neurodesign Can Do for You
As demonstrated in Erin's story, the neurodesign philosophy draws from the psychology of art and design to create environments where people can thrive, whether it's a home, a workspace, or a commercial enterprise. While most good designers and architects work with their clients' objectives in mind, neurodesign takes the process a step further and addresses the deeper psychological needs that present as issues in the living environment, allowing neurodesigners to create spaces that are natural extensions of our clients' lifestyles.

Neurodesign can be applied to any scenario where the design environment comes into play. Whether you are a designer or planner who wants to create spaces that address your client's psychological needs, someone looking for a new space to live or work, a couple moving in together, a family planning a renovation, or an adult considering moving an aging parent into their home, you can apply these principles.

Imagine stepping into your home and feeling an immediate sense of peace, focus, and connection—a space that not only shelters you but actively supports your well-being, relationships, and aspirations. This is the promise of neurodesign.

In a world where we spend so much time at home, the design of our spaces has never been more critical. Neurodesign empowers you to create a home that works *with* you, not against you. It's about turning your environment into an ally that boosts your creativity, helps you recharge, fosters meaningful connections, and transforms your daily routines.

The next chapter will dive deeper into how neuroscience, psychology, and design principles come together to create spaces that inspire and support. Whether you are looking to reduce stress, deepen relationships, or create a home that feels genuinely *yours,* neurodesign offers the tools to make it possible. Your home has the potential to be more than a physical structure—it can be a sanctuary for growth, harmony, and transformation.

3

The Harmonious Home: Emotional, Physical, and Spiritual Well-Being

A. Quincy Jones was a visionary architect who designed for emotional, physical, and spiritual well-being. When I was staging an A. Quincy Jones-designed home in Los Angeles, I knew his architecture spoke to neurodesign principles—the circular layout, high ceilings that inspired a spiritual sense of awe, access to biophilia, connection to greenery, lighting from skylights, the grounding of the earth and stone, and a conversation pit encouraging connection and belonging, while supporting privacy and intimacy in windows and rooms that were adaptable to provide balance in both. The harmonious home became a metaphor for how psychological health and home intersect in Maslow's hierarchy of the harmonious home.

The Harmonious Home: Maslow's Hierarchy

Maslow's hierarchy of needs is a psychological theory introduced by Abraham Maslow that suggests human beings are motivated by a series of hierarchical needs. At the pyramid's base are physiological needs essential for survival, such as food, water, and shelter. Once these basic needs are met, individuals can focus on safety needs, which include personal security, employment, and health. The next level, love and belonging, emphasizes the importance of relationships, friendships, and a sense of connection with others. Following this are esteem needs, which involve the desire for respect, recognition, and a sense of accomplishment. Finally, at the top of the hierarchy is self-actualization, which represents fulfilling one's potential, creativity, and personal growth. Maslow's hierarchy of needs is closely related to the concept of a "harmonious home" because a home can provide the foundation for meeting many of these basic and psychological needs essential for emotional and physical health. At the most basic level, a harmonious home ensures that physiological needs—comfort, warmth, and access to necessities like food, water, and sleep—are met. The design and environment of a home can have a big impact on one's ability to feel physically and emotionally secure, thereby supporting safety needs. This can be achieved by living in a secure home, a safe neighborhood, and a nurturing environment that provides stability and protection (Maslow 1943).

A harmonious home also addresses the higher levels of Maslow's hierarchy, such as belonging, esteem, and self-actualization. Spaces that encourage connection—whether through shared living areas, spaces for family interaction, or private spaces for relaxation—help fulfill the need for love and belonging. A home can nurture self-esteem and promote self-actualization by incorporating elements that support creativity, personal growth, and accomplishment. The design of a harmonious home that emphasizes balance, mindfulness, and connection to nature can help individuals achieve their highest potential and support overall mental, emotional, and physical health.

Maslow's hierarchy has influenced psychology, education, and business, providing a framework for understanding human motivation and personal development. We will explore Maslow's hierarchy of needs as it relates to neurodesign more deeply in Chapter 5. We will further introduce the harmonious home as a place for self and relationship actualization, as shown in the diagram here:

Neurodesign Harmonious Home Hierarchy

The Harmonious Home: A Story of Renewal and Connection

Sarah and Kevin Thompson never imagined their home would be central to their healing journey. After a difficult year of financial stress, health challenges, and the death of Sarah's mother, their once-happy family felt fractured. The house that had been a backdrop for so many joyful memories now seemed heavy with tension and sadness. Conversations were strained, daily routines felt chaotic, and their connection to one another had weakened under the weight of their struggles.

Determined to find a way forward, Sarah began researching how their environment might influence their well-being. She discovered the concept of "the harmonious home," an approach that sees home as a sanctuary for emotional, physical, and spiritual health. Inspired, she proposed transforming their space to support their journey toward healing. The family was initially skeptical, but they agreed it was time for a change.

Emotional Healing: Spaces for Connection and Comfort
The first step was creating areas where they could reconnect. They started with the heart of their home—the living room. They replaced the bulky furniture with a cozy sectional, added soft blankets, and positioned the seating to encourage face-to-face conversations. Sarah hung family photos and mementos on the walls, creating a visual narrative of their family life.

They also implemented a nightly ritual called "family reset," where they gathered in their new space to share highlights of their day. These moments helped them rebuild trust and strengthen emotional bonds.

Physical Well-Being: A Healthier Environment
To support physical health, the Thompsons tackled their cluttered kitchen. Understanding that disorganized environments can contribute to stress and poor eating habits, they reorganized it with intention. Fresh produce became the centerpiece of their center island, replacing sugary snacks. They reorganized their pantry and clearly labeled containers, making finding ingredients and preparing meals as a family easier.

The bedrooms were also updated. They replaced harsh lighting with warm, dimmable options and chose soothing colors like soft blues and greens. These changes helped everyone sleep better, which improved their moods.

Spiritual Renewal: Creating Sacred Spaces
For spiritual well-being, each family member got a little space to turn into their personal sanctuary. Sarah set up a meditation area in a sunlit corner of the bedroom by adding a yoga mat, candles, and a small fountain for soothing background noise. Kevin created a music nook where he could play his guitar. The children, Emily and Jack, turned their playroom into a space for creativity, decorating it with art supplies and a dream board for their aspirations.

As a family, they remade their backyard into a peaceful retreat. They planted a garden with flowers and vegetables that symbolized their journey. This shared project not only provided fresh air and physical activity but also became a living testament to their resilience and growth.

The Transformation
As the months passed, the Thompsons' house began to feel like a home again—a place of comfort, joy, and renewal. Their family rituals deepened their emotional bonds, while the calming spaces allowed each member to recharge in their own way. Most importantly, the home reflected who they were and what they valued: love, resilience, and hope.

The Thompsons' journey demonstrates that a home is far more than four walls and a roof. When approached with intention, it can become a sanctuary where emotional, physical, and spiritual well-being can thrive.

The Science Behind the Healing Environment
As a licensed psychotherapist with my niche in coaching/consulting in the neurodesign methodology, I have experienced firsthand how

my clients' need for healing and growth is reflected in their relationships and environment. I have seen their lives transform once they embrace a systems approach to designing with intention focused on their needs. Although most good designers and architects are already doing this in their practice, I take it a step further by intervening as a psychotherapist and incorporating the deeper psychological needs in design while mediating relationships facing obstacles in their living situations.

Emotional Well-being: An intentional space that integrates design elements based on environmental psychology can significantly elevate emotional wellness. Factors like lighting, color, texture, and flow can calm the nervous system and reduce stress. Incorporating natural light, soft hues, and organic textures can promote a sense of calm, helping occupants feel at peace within their homes. A space carefully curated to reflect personal tastes and values enhances feelings of safety and contentment and provides emotional grounding.

Relationship Dynamics: Intentional spaces can be a catalyst for meaningful social connections. Living environments designed with environmental psychology in mind can encourage interactions that deepen relationships. Open layouts, for example, can bring families together and promote communication, while thoughtfully designed private spaces bring the balance needed for autonomy and reflection. Harmonious home environments can provide the setting for positive family interactions and improved relationship dynamics.

Cognitive Health: An artfully designed space can also support cognitive health by reducing cognitive load and enhancing focus and creativity. Clutter-free, organized environments help minimize distractions, leading to more mental clarity and productivity. Incorporating elements of nature through biophilic design, such as plants, natural light, or water features, has been shown to improve cognitive function, boost creativity, and reduce symptoms of mental fatigue (Kellert and Calabrese 2015). These spaces encourage rest, rejuvenation, and mental focus, which are essential for navigating life's complexities.

Attachment to Place: Artful design can enhance attachment to one's home by creating a personal and meaningful space. Research shows that people who love their homes experience greater satisfaction and happiness, leading to better mental health and stronger family relationships.

Ultimately, harmonious living is not just about creating visually appealing homes; it's also about crafting environments that nourish the body, mind, and spirit. By thoughtfully curating our living spaces and adopting environmental psychology principles, we can live more intentionally, achieve emotional balance, and experience richer, more fulfilling relationships.

What the Research Says About Neuroscience

The contribution of science is also a central tenet in how to live harmoniously in that we fundamentally can benefit from understanding how we live in our surroundings. This knowledge is based on understanding our perception of our environment, our working memory, and how our bodies move, navigate, and are mirrored in space. Research into how neuroscience informs building and architecture to create living environments that promote wellness and health has become increasingly prevalent.

Several foundations I'm a member of have neuroscientists and architects devoted to creating thoughtful dialogues about how neuroscience can inform design. For instance, the Academy of Neuroscience for Architecture (ANFA) was formed in 2002 as a legacy project of the National Institute of Architects (AIA) to promote and advance knowledge that links neuroscience to the built environment.

While we often assume good design involves an understanding of how people live and navigate space, furthering this dialogue can only strengthen the support for wellness in our living environment.

For example, understanding the functions of implicit and explicit memory, short-term and long-term memory, and their role in design choices—like why we choose a tree-lined street that reminds us of our childhood or art that reminds us of scenes our elders loved—can help us understand how an individual diagnosed with dementia navigates their space in the short term to meet their immediate needs to reduce psychological distress. Briefly, implicit and explicit memory are both forms of long-term memory. While implicit memory recalls unconscious material more automatically, explicit memory takes conscious effort to remember. The classic example of listening to music and singing the words of a song naturally requires implicit memory, but recalling a to-do list would call upon explicit memory.

Sensory input from our living environment directly influences our neurobiology and shapes how our brain and body respond to the space around us. When we encounter different stimuli—such as light, sound, texture, or scent—our nervous system processes these signals, affecting how we feel and behave in that space. For instance, natural or soft, warm lighting can trigger the release of serotonin, a neurotransmitter that promotes a sense of well-being and happiness. In contrast, harsh or fluorescent lighting may increase cortisol levels, the stress hormone, making us anxious or on edge (Kandel and Schwartz 2012).

Sounds also play a critical role in shaping our neurobiological responses. Pleasant, gentle sounds, like the rustling of leaves or calming music, can activate the parasympathetic nervous system, which helps us relax. On the other hand, loud or jarring noises can activate the sympathetic nervous system, which triggers the "fight or flight" response, making us feel stressed, hyperalert, or uneasy. Textures we touch, such as soft fabrics, smooth surfaces, or rough materials, also affect the brain. Positive tactile experiences, like touching a soft blanket or smooth wood, can stimulate the release of oxytocin, a hormone linked to feelings of safety and comfort.

Conversely, uncomfortable or irritating textures might increase physical tension or unease (Eagleman 2015). Scents have a direct route to the brain's limbic system, which controls emotions and memory. Pleasant scents, like lavender or citrus, can calm the nervous system and promote relaxation, while unpleasant odors can activate stress responses or trigger negative memories (S. Chou and M. Chou 2023).

These sensory experiences interact with our brain's emotional and survival centers, like the amygdala and hippocampus, influencing our mood and how we associate spaces with safety or stress. Over time, environments rich in positive sensory input can help regulate the nervous system, promote healing, and improve mental health, whereas spaces with negative sensory cues may contribute to heightened stress, anxiety, or even trauma responses. In this way, the sensory experience of our living environment profoundly impacts our neurobiology, shaping how we feel, behave, and connect with the world around us (Murthy 2015).

While neuroscience and architecture are two separate disciplines, an increasingly scholastic dialogue is bringing these two fields together. In Eberhard's (2008) book, *Brain Landscape: The Coexistence of Neuroscience and Architecture,* he proposed how the knowledge of neuroscience can aid in stress reduction, improved cognition, productivity, spirituality, and emotional responses. Further examples of neuroscience meeting architecture can be found in the seminal book *When Brains Meet Buildings* (Airbib 2020). In this book, Airbib breaks down the neuroscience of our brains and touches on the brain functions of memory and perception and how they can be applied to the built environment. He emphasizes the importance of designers understanding the brain's functions and argues that knowledge of brain matter and function is as critical for design as knowing the properties of materials like steel, concrete, and glass fiber (Airbib 2020). This knowledge enables designers to make more informed, effective decisions in creating environments that affect human cognition and behavior.

It has become increasingly beneficial for neuroscience to apply its knowledge of how environment affects the brain, as Ibrahim (2019) asserts in his research. Neuroscientists study how the brain processes sensation, perception, decision-making, and emotion, including how we interact with and navigate our environment, perceive, store, and recall sensory information, and how we react to different situations. In contrast, the emerging field of neuroarchitecture focuses on how aspects of the built environment, like light, space, and layout, impact physical and psychological wellness. This field explores how these elements influence brain functions related to stress, emotion, and memory (Ibrahim 2019).

In neurodesign, the goal is to increase wellness, creativity, and productivity in our living spaces, and applying neuroscience to our design choices can only maximize these goals.

Some design principles that support neurological wellness in living spaces include:

- Incorporating boundaries or openness in a floor plan. For example, sliding glass doors can promote indoor-outdoor flexibility to align with sympathetic nervous system responses such as feeling trapped (heart racing, perspiring) or needing containment (feeling lost, ungrounded).
- Situating office furniture to face a window so you can watch trees sway can help orient and calm the nervous system. Similarly, placing an office chair to face the door so you can see who's coming toward you can calm the primitive fight-or-flight response.
- Incorporating lighting design and using dimmers that can align with the body's circadian rhythms or help with seasonal affective disorder.

- Painting a room with a color that gauges the mood and function of the room. For example, use yellow in a kitchen to help you wake up and feel stimulated, and apply red to promote passion and activation.

What Is Neuroarchitecture?
Imagine walking into a warm and cozy room and instantly feeling calm—your shoulders relax, your breathing slows, and your mind clears. Now, picture stepping into a different space that feels chaotic and overwhelming, leaving you feeling tense and distracted. These reactions are not random. They are your brain responding to the environment around you, and this is where neuroarchitecture comes in.

Neuroarchitecture is the science of designing spaces that align with how our brains work and creating environments that support our emotional, mental, and physical wellness. It is a multidisciplinary approach that combines neuroscience, psychology, architecture, and design to craft spaces that look and *feel* good.

For example, have you ever noticed how natural light streaming through a window can lift your spirits? Or how a cluttered room can make you anxious? Neuroarchitecture takes these observations and grounds them in science. Research shows that sunlight triggers the release of serotonin, improving mood and focus, while clutter increases cognitive overload, making it harder to concentrate. Neuroarchitecture supports creating spaces that promote clarity, relaxation, and connection by understanding how design elements like light, color, sound, and layout affect our brains.

But neuroarchitecture goes beyond just personal comfort—it also builds stronger relationships and enhances productivity. In workplaces, thoughtful design can boost creativity and collaboration; in homes, it can strengthen family bonds and create harmony. A well-designed home office might use biophilic principles by incorporating plants and natural textures to reduce stress and increase focus. And a kitchen with ergonomic flow and warm lighting can encourage meaningful mealtime conversations.

At its heart, neuroarchitecture asks a simple yet profound question: How can the spaces we inhabit make us healthier, happier, and more connected? Whether it's a hospital designed to promote healing, a school built to enhance learning, or a home crafted for peace and connection, neuroarchitecture bridges the gap between science and design to create spaces that truly support the people who live and work within them. It is a revolution in how we think about the built environment, proving that good design is not just about aesthetics—it's about shaping how we feel, think, and thrive.

What Is Neuroaesthetics?
Have you ever walked into a room and immediately felt at peace, perhaps overwhelmed by the beauty of the space or the design of the surroundings? Maybe you've listened to a song that resonated deeply, causing an emotional response, or observed a work of art that stirred something within you. These moments are not just subjective experiences—they are at the heart of a field of study known as neuroaesthetics. Neuroaesthetics is the science of how we perceive and respond to beauty, art, and design and how these aesthetic experiences influence our emotions and cognition. It combines principles of neuroscience, psychology, and aesthetics to uncover the biological and cognitive processes behind our appreciation for beauty.

At the heart of neuroaesthetics is the recognition that our brains are wired to respond to certain visual, auditory, and sensory stimuli in particular ways. For instance, when we experience beauty, whether in nature, art, or design, our brains respond by releasing feel-good chemicals like dopamine and serotonin. This neurological reaction is deeply rooted in how our brains process visual and sensory information. Neuroaesthetics helps us understand these processes and provides insights into how beauty affects our well-being in tangible, measurable ways.

The Science Behind Neuroaesthetics
Neuroaesthetics seeks to explain why specific designs, artworks, or environments resonate with us so deeply and emotionally. One of the most significant discoveries in neuroaesthetics is the role of the brain's reward centers, specifically the orbitofrontal cortex, in processing beauty. The orbitofrontal cortex is part of the brain involved in decision-making, reward processing, and experiencing pleasure. Research has shown that when we encounter aesthetically pleasing stimuli, whether in art, nature, or design, this area of the brain is activated and releases dopamine, a neurotransmitter that plays a key role in feelings of pleasure and reward (Zeki 1999). This process is not limited to art alone—it extends to the built environment, including architecture, interior design, and urban spaces, all of which can have a profound impact on how we feel. The connection between beauty and well-being is not simply a matter of individual taste or cultural influences; it's a biological response to stimuli that the brain interprets as positive or rewarding.

For example, when we view a symmetrical object, such as a well-proportioned sculpture or a harmonious color palette, the brain's reward centers respond more strongly than when we look at something that appears chaotic or asymmetrical. This reaction extends to the natural world as well. Symmetry and balance are often found in natural forms, such as flowers, trees, and landscapes, which is why we find these forms inherently pleasing.

Fractals: Patterns Found in Nature
Fractals—repetitive and self-similar patterns across different scales found in nature, such as the branching of trees or the shape of

mountain ranges—are another example of universally pleasing aesthetics. Studies have shown that gazing at fractal patterns triggers positive emotional responses and is associated with reduced stress and increased relaxation (Berto 2005).

The preference for symmetry and fractals and the brain's ease in processing these patterns have significant implications for design. By incorporating these elements into architecture, interior design, and urban planning, designers can create spaces that improve both emotional well-being and cognitive function. Whether in healthcare environments, public spaces, or homes, the strategic use of symmetry and natural patterns can have a profound effect on how we feel and function in those spaces.

Practical Applications of Neuroaesthetics

Neuroaesthetics has far-reaching applications across various fields, from healthcare to urban planning to interior design. Understanding how beauty affects our brains allows us to design spaces that look good and actively improve our mental and physical health. One of the most significant areas where neuroaesthetics has had an impact is in healthcare design. Hospitals designed with aesthetic principles—such as soft, calming colors, natural materials, and artwork—can speed up recovery and reduce patient stress. Patient rooms that incorporate elements like nature views, natural light, and soothing colors have been found to reduce anxiety, lower blood pressure, and even shorten the duration of hospitalization.

Incorporating aesthetic elements in healthcare spaces is not just about decoration but also about creating environments that promote healing. The calming effects of nature-inspired design are significant in hospitals, where patients are often experiencing stress, fear, or discomfort. Healthcare facilities can create environments that support the healing process and improve patient outcomes by designing spaces that evoke calm and peace. For example, studies have shown that patients who recover in rooms with natural views or access to gardens tend to heal faster and require less pain medication. These findings highlight the tangible benefits of integrating neuroaesthetic principles into the design of healthcare environments (Ulrich 1984).

Urban planning has also shifted toward incorporating neuroaesthetic principles. Public spaces that include greenery, flowing water, and visually harmonious designs can encourage relaxation, reduce stress, and promote social interaction. Parks, plazas, and streetscapes that prioritize aesthetic qualities not only improve a city's physical appearance but also the mental and emotional well-being of the people who use them. Green spaces, in particular, have been linked to reduced stress and improved mood, making them essential components of any urban environment (Hartig et al. 2003).

Applying neuroaesthetic principles in our homes can be just as transformative. From the colors on the walls to the furniture and décor textures, every element contributes to how we feel. Bright lighting can increase energy levels and focus, soft textures can evoke comfort and warmth, and complex surfaces may make us more alert and focused. By consciously choosing these materials based on how they resonate with our emotional state, we can create living spaces that are both functional and emotionally supportive.

The Connection Between Aesthetic Experience and Well-Being

At its core, neuroaesthetics helps us understand the connection between beauty and well-being. Beauty is not just a subjective experience; it has a biological basis that shapes how we respond to the world. How our brains react to beauty—whether through visual art, music, or design—reveals that our appreciation for aesthetics is rooted in evolutionary processes shaped by biology. This connection between beauty and well-being is essential in understanding how we can design environments that make us feel better, not just aesthetically but emotionally and psychologically.

Neuroaesthetics has shown that our brains respond to certain aesthetic elements in ways that directly influence our mental health. By applying the principles of neuroaesthetics, we can create environments that not only look good but actively contribute to our emotional and psychological wellness. Understanding how beauty affects the brain in healthcare, urban spaces, and homes allows us to design environments that support healing, relaxation, and positive emotions. Whether it's the calming effect of a symmetrical room, the restorative power of natural patterns, or the soothing impact of natural light and color, neuroaesthetics provides a powerful tool for creating spaces that promote well-being.

A Methodology for Transformation
The neurodesign methodology is not just about creating beautiful spaces—it is about crafting environments that reflect who we are, support who we want to become, and enrich our lives at every level. By combining structured methods with curiosity, exploration, and evidence-based design, neurodesign empowers individuals to transform their spaces into places of purpose, meaning, and connection.

Neurodesign Methodology: Transforming Spaces with Purpose
The neurodesign methodology is a comprehensive, research-driven approach that bridges psychology, neuroscience, and design to create environments that support emotional, physical, and relational well-being. At its heart lies the neurodesign method, a structured yet dynamic framework for designing spaces with intention and care. Below are the steps that make up that framework.

The Neurodesign Method: Structured Steps for Meaningful Change

1. **Interview/Assessment:**
   The process begins with an in-depth exploration of the inhabitant's relationship with their environment. During the interview, clients share their current emotional, functional, and aesthetic experiences regarding their space. Questions explore how they feel in their home right now, what memories or feelings are tied to specific spaces, and how the environment aligns (or misaligns) with their values and goals. This phase creates a foundation for understanding their unique needs and aspirations.

2. **Plan/Goals:**
   Based on the assessment, clear and actionable goals are developed. These may include facilitating better family communication, creating a space that inspires creativity, or designing rooms that support relaxation and healing. This stage involves integrating design principles like color psychology, wayfinding, and ergonomics with the client's specific objectives.

3. **Intervention:**
   The intervention phase is where the transformation of the space takes place. Design strategies are implemented to address emotional and functional needs. This could include introducing biophilic elements, such as indoor plants and natural light, reorganizing layouts to improve flow, or showcasing personal artifacts to enhance connection and meaning. The goal is to create a space that reflects the client's identity and supports their goals.

4. **Maintenance:**
    Spaces evolve over time, and so do the people who inhabit them. The final phase focuses on maintaining the intentionality of the design. Regular check-ins and adaptations ensure the space remains aligned with the inhabitant's changing needs, supporting long-term harmony and growth.

Exercises: Connecting with Place and Memory
The neurodesign methodology incorporates exercises to deepen the inhabitants' connection to their space and help uncover emotional insights that guide the design. These exercises include:

- **Timeline of Home:** Clients map out the significant spaces they've lived in throughout their lives to identify patterns of attachment or discomfort and reflect on what each environment contributed to their sense of self.
- **Childhood Home Visualization:** Clients recall their childhood home, focusing on its sights, sounds, smells, and feelings. This exercise often reveals emotional connections to elements like light, color, or spatial arrangements, which can inform the new design.
- **Connection to Place-Object:** Clients identify meaningful objects or areas in their current home and explore why these items resonate with them. This process helps them define what should be preserved or emphasized in the new design.

Curiosity, Exploration, and Experimentation:
Pathways to Transformation
Central to the methodology is the belief that transformation is a discovery process. By encouraging curiosity, clients can explore unconventional ideas and experiment with their space. This may involve rearranging furniture, trying out different color palettes, or introducing

sensory elements like soundscapes or scents. These small tweaks build confidence and provide immediate feedback on what works, making the transformation deeply personal and impactful.

Room as Function: Designing for Outcomes
Every room serves a purpose, and design strategy is key to achieving desired outcomes. By employing evidence-based research, neurodesign ensures that spaces support their intended function:

- **Workspaces:** A focus on ergonomic furniture, ample natural light, and biophilic design improves focus and productivity.
- **Bedrooms:** Featuring soothing colors, blackout curtains, and soundproofing promotes restful sleep.
- **Living Rooms:** Circular seating arrangements, warm lighting, and personal artifacts create more opportunity for connection and communication.
- **Kitchens:** Open layouts, functional flow, and vibrant colors encourage creativity and ensure that the kitchen is the hub of the house.

Room Function and Intention
Just as the home plays out relational dynamics, the home holds symbolism and shared meaning for each room, each with its own purpose, function, and value. Every room has a historical reference point, an architectural anchoring, and a symbolic gesture, which we explore in detail in case studies throughout the book that feature people who imbued their homes with purpose, intention, and meaning. How we relate to our lover in the bedroom can differ depending on the need for sleep or intimacy, as does how we commune in our dining area when we want to relax with a glass of wine or eat. Sometimes, rooms hold the paradoxes of life, while intentional design can act strategically to meet the needs of an individual, dyad,

and family system. The places in our home where we work, play, eat, connect, rest, sustain, and create all have a shared design purpose.

Living Room: Social Connection and Relaxation. The living room is typically the main gathering area for social interaction and bonding. Comfortable seating, natural light, and calming colors can make this space ideal for unwinding and nurturing positive relationships.

Kitchen: Creativity and Nourishment. As the heart of the home, the kitchen is where meals are prepared, nourishing both body and mind. Cooking can be a creative outlet and stress reliever, while shared meals promote connection. Incorporating windows, plants, or colors like greens and warm yellows can create a welcoming and energizing space.

Bedroom: Rest and Restoration. The bedroom should be a sanctuary for sleep and relaxation, with features like blackout curtains, soft lighting, and soothing colors. Restricting screen time in the bedroom and adding calming elements can support restorative sleep, which is essential for emotional regulation and mental health.

Bathroom: Self-Care and Mindfulness. The bathroom offers a private space for personal care routines, supporting self-nurturing habits that can boost self-esteem. Adding elements like plants, soft lighting, or aromatherapy can enhance relaxation and create a spa-like atmosphere that encourages mindfulness.

Home Office: Productivity and Focus. An organized and designated workspace with natural light, ergonomic furniture, and minimal distractions supports productivity and focus. Setting boundaries for this area can aid work-life balance, helping reduce stress and improve mental clarity.

Dining Room: Ritual and Routine. A separate dining area encourages mindful eating and shared family rituals, which help establish structure. Regular shared meals here can reinforce routine, reduce stress, promote connection, and offer emotional stability.

Entryway: Transition and Preparation. The entryway is a transition point, symbolizing a shift from the outside world to your personal sanctuary. Simple organization and calming colors help ease the transition between environments, setting a positive tone as one enters or exits.

Outdoor Space (Garden or Balcony): Nature and Tranquility. Outdoor areas provide a place to connect with nature, which is known to reduce stress and improve mood. With a few plants, natural sunlight, or a quiet seating area, even small spaces can benefit mental health by serving as a retreat for relaxation and grounding.

When each area is purposefully designed to balance psychological support with function, it can meet distinct mental health needs.

The Intersection of Design and Health
The ability of good design to improve health is not just anecdotal; it is supported by decades of research and a growing body of evidence in environmental psychology, neuroscience, and architecture. Ecological psychology and neuroscience studies consistently show that spaces designed with intention—incorporating natural light, greenery, color psychology, and spatial flow—can lower cortisol levels, enhance mental clarity, and improve overall wellness. As we continue to evolve our understanding, we are increasingly aware of the power that design holds in shaping not just the aesthetic quality of our surroundings but also our physiological and psychological health.

Environmental psychology, a field that studies the relationship between humans and their physical surroundings, has long argued that the spaces we inhabit have a profound impact on us. Studies began to emerge in the 1980s showing that the built environment could influence both our physical health and our mental state. Researchers like Stephen Kaplan and Rachel Kaplan (1989) conducted pioneering work that demonstrated the restorative effects of nature. This research highlighted the profound connection between the natural environment and human well-being, suggesting that our bodies and brains respond positively to environments that replicate natural patterns and promote opportunities for relaxation and restoration.

One of the most influential studies in this area was conducted by Roger Ulrich (1984), which examined the impact of natural views on patients recovering from surgery. Ulrich's groundbreaking study found that hospital patients who had rooms with windows that offered views of nature healed faster and required less pain medication than those in rooms without natural views. The study's findings not only provided empirical evidence that nature has therapeutic benefits but also sparked increased interest in biophilic design. Ulrich's work, along with the Kaplans' studies, helped shift the perspective on design from being merely functional to being a vital tool for improving health outcomes. This research has since been replicated in various contexts and has confirmed that even small interactions with nature, such as exposure to natural light, the presence of plants, or access to outdoor spaces, can have a significant positive impact on health. More recent studies have expanded on the work of Kaplan and Kaplan and Ulrich, further corroborating the importance of design in health. Research on color psychology, for example, has shown that color can influence our mood, productivity, and even physiological states.

Research in neuroscience has also provided insights into the biological mechanisms that underlie the relationship between environment and well-being. Studies on the brain's response to environmental stimuli have demonstrated that exposure to natural elements can reduce stress by lowering cortisol levels, the hormone associated with stress and anxiety. A study conducted by van den Berg et al. (2003) found that individuals who spent time in green spaces had lower cortisol levels and reported feeling less stressed. These findings support the idea that our physical environment can directly influence our brain chemistry, leading to measurable changes in our mood and stress levels.

Beyond just nature, the design of the space itself—how it is arranged, lit, and experienced—can also play a significant role in how we feel and behave. Spatial flow, which refers to the way rooms and furniture are arranged to facilitate movement and interaction, can either support or undermine our well-being. Poor spatial flow can lead to feeling frustrated, claustrophobic, and stressed, whereas spaces that are thoughtfully designed to facilitate ease of movement, connection, and access to natural light can produce a sense of calm and openness.

The idea of "prospect and refuge," a theory developed by the environmental psychologist Jay Appleton (1975), is particularly relevant in understanding the role of spatial flow in well-being. According to this theory, people are drawn to environments where they feel protected and can observe their surroundings. Spaces that have a good balance between openness (prospect) and privacy (refuge) are often perceived as more comfortable and secure, which is why elements like windows, open views, and areas of seclusion are so important in designing spaces that support health. Whether it's a home, a workplace, or a hospital room, incorporating principles of prospect and refuge can enhance feelings of safety and control, which in turn reduces stress and anxiety.

As more research continues to emerge, it is becoming increasingly clear that integrating nature, color, spatial flow, and other design elements into our built environments has a measurable impact on our health. The growing field of neuroarchitecture, which combines neuroscience, psychology, and design, continues to push the boundaries of what we know about how the built environment influences our physical and emotional states. By applying principles of biophilic design, ergonomic planning, and sensory integration, designers are creating spaces that not only meet functional needs but also promote healing, productivity, and happiness.

In environmental psychology, the living space is not merely a backdrop to human life but a dynamic force that shapes emotions, behaviors, and overall wellness. The design of a space can either nurture or hinder mental health. A well-designed environment that considers light, color, texture, and spatial arrangement has the power to provide safety, comfort, and empowerment. Ultimately, the living space is a powerful tool in crafting an individual's sense of self, shaping experiences that either elevate or confine us.

Let's explore why good design is good for our health and the psychological theory that supports this.

Designing for Health: How Thoughtful Spaces Transform Lives

When Lisa moved into her new apartment, she had not anticipated that the space would have such a dramatic impact on her well-being. For years, she had struggled with chronic stress and mild depression. Her previous apartment was dark, cluttered, and uninspiring, leaving her feeling drained and unmotivated. But her new apartment, designed by an architect heavily influenced by biophilic principles, was entirely different.

The apartment's design intentionally balanced natural light, open spaces, and carefully chosen materials. Floor-to-ceiling windows allowed sunlight to flood the living area, while strategically placed plants added beauty and life. A skylight above the kitchen created a direct connection to the changing light throughout the day, which subtly reinforced her circadian rhythms. Within weeks, Lisa noticed the difference: she was in a better mood, had more energy, and felt more focused and alive.

Lessons from Visionary Architects

Throughout history, architects have shaped more than just skylines and landscapes—they have shaped the way we live, breathe, and find balance within our homes. From the early modernists to contemporary pioneers, the greatest minds in architecture have understood that a home is more than four walls; it is a space that should nurture physical and mental health, encourage creativity, and provide refuge from the chaos of the outside world.

One of the earliest champions of health-driven architecture was Richard Neutra, a pioneer of modernism who believed architectural design should enhance human vitality. His 1929 Lovell Health House in Los Angeles was revolutionary—not just for its steel-framed construction but for its seamless integration of air, light, and nature. Long before the principles of biophilic design were widely recognized, Neutra believed that access to fresh air, natural light, and open space could improve physical health and mental clarity. His work still influences contemporary architecture, particularly in the way living spaces are designed to connect occupants to the natural world (Hines 2006).

Building on the idea of integrating nature into everyday life, Frank Lloyd Wright became one of the most influential figures in American architecture. His Prairie-style homes, and later his masterpiece, Fallingwater, designed in 1935, embodied his philosophy of organic architecture—designing structures that exist in harmony with their surroundings. Fallingwater, which features cascading terraces and overhanging balconies perched above a rushing waterfall, is a striking example of how architecture can evoke a sense of serenity and inspiration. Wright believed that living in spaces closely tied to nature could enhance well-being, a philosophy now widely supported by environmental psychology and biophilic research (McCarter 2006).

Across the Atlantic, Le Corbusier was pioneering a different philosophy. His 1931 Villa Savoye exemplified the principles of modernist architecture: clean lines, open floor plans, and a deep commitment to efficiency. "A house is a machine for living in," he famously stated (Le Corbusier 1986, 87). His belief that architecture should be functional, light-filled, and open-air laid the foundation for many of today's wellness-focused homes, where simplicity and natural elements promote clarity and serenity.

As architecture evolved into the late 20th century, the idea that a home should serve as a retreat gained even more traction. Tadao Ando, a Japanese architect known for his mastery of concrete and light, created spaces that encourage mindfulness and reflection. His Row House in Sumiyoshi is a prime example—using thoughtfully designed courtyards and attention to shadows and natural light to create an environment that brings inner peace. Ando's philosophy of "wabi-sabi," which embraces simplicity and imperfection, continues to inspire minimalist home design today (Ando 2012).

While Ando focused on serenity, Peter Zumthor explored the sensory experience of architecture. His designs, such as the Therme Vals spa in Switzerland, use raw materials, strategic lighting, and spatial flow to engage the senses and create a deeply immersive experience. His approach reminds us that the way we move through a home—how it feels, sounds, and even smells—affects our well-being as much as its appearance (Zumthor 1999).

In recent decades, architects have expanded their focus beyond aesthetics and tranquility to include social responsibility and adaptability. Alejandro Aravena, for example, has reimagined affordable housing. His Quinta Monroy project in Chile gives residents a chance to build onto pre-designed structures, creating flexible, expandable homes that evolve with their inhabitants' needs. His work challenges the notion that good design is a luxury and emphasizes that architecture should be accessible and adaptable for all (Aravena 2016).

Similarly, Shigeru Ban has revolutionized humanitarian architecture by designing homes that are not only affordable but also sustainable. His Paper Log House, created as a temporary housing solution for people displaced by natural disasters, demonstrates how design can provide dignity, comfort, and psychological security for displaced communities. Ban's commitment to using recyclable materials and modular construction proves that innovation and empathy can coexist in residential design (Jodidio 2014).

Another innovator, Jeanne Gang, has challenged the traditional high-rise model with her Aqua Tower in Chicago, designed to maximize outdoor space and social interaction. By incorporating undulating balconies and shared spaces, she redefined what urban residential living could be—a balance of privacy, nature, and community (Gang 2017).

Tatiana Bilbao, a rising force in architecture, focuses on blending cultural heritage with modern adaptability. Her modular housing projects allow homeowners to expand their living spaces gradually, reflecting how families grow and change over time. Her designs emphasize that a home should be more than a fixed structure; it should be a space that's allowed to evolve to meet the needs of its inhabitants throughout the different stages of their lives (Bilbao 2019).

Bjarke Ingels, known for his concept of "hedonistic sustainability," has redefined contemporary living spaces by proving that environmentally responsible homes can still be exciting and bold. His Mountain Dwellings in Copenhagen feature tiered apartments with lush green rooftops, blending urban living with the benefits of nature. Ingels's designs challenge the idea that sustainability requires sacrifice, instead promoting homes that are as enjoyable as they are eco-friendly (Ingels 2011).

Most recently, Michael Murphy, co-founder of MASS Design Group in Boston, has led the charge in health-focused architecture.

His work designing hospitals and residential spaces prioritizes air circulation, natural light, and spatial flow and proves that design can have measurable effects on health outcomes. His Butaro District Hospital in Rwanda, with its open corridors and nature-infused spaces, exemplifies how architecture can be a tool for healing (Murphy and Gutman 2020).

From Neutra's belief in the science of well-being to Wright's organic harmony, from Ando's meditative simplicity to Aravena's flexible housing, the greatest architects have always recognized that a home is more than shelter—it is a space that shapes the lives of those who dwell within it. Whether through natural materials, flexible design, or innovative sustainability, these visionaries remind us that our environments are not passive backdrops but active participants in our well-being.

A Better Future Through Design
Lisa's experience with her new apartment and the legacies of Wright, Le Corbusier, and Murphy demonstrate a universal truth: Good design is more than aesthetics—it is a tool for health, happiness, and resilience. Looking ahead, the integration of neurodesign principles is pushing the boundaries of what is possible in architecture and interior spaces. With a greater understanding of how spatial organization, lighting, color, and materials affect the brain, designers can create environments that improve productivity, relaxation, and emotional balance. Studies in environmental psychology suggest that intentional design elements can significantly impact mental health outcomes and strengthen social bonds.

Furthermore, technological advances are making it easier than ever to craft adaptable, responsive spaces that cater to individual needs. Smart homes equipped with AI-driven environmental controls can personalize lighting, temperature, and acoustics. Innovations in biophilic design, including living walls, indoor gardens, and sustainable materials, are helping residents reconnect with nature, even in urban environments. By incorporating these elements, architects are designing homes that not only serve as shelters but also actively contribute to health and happiness.

Beyond the personal benefits, well-designed environments also strengthen communities. Thoughtfully designed public spaces encourage social interaction and physical activity. Walkable neighborhoods with green spaces and mixed-use developments create opportunities for engagement, which reduces isolation and enhances quality of life. Research underscores that individuals who live in well-planned communities report higher levels of happiness and social cohesion, proving that design has the power to shape not just individual health but also communal health.

Ultimately, the future of design lies in its ability to create holistic environments that support every aspect of our lives. By embracing evidence-based practices and forward-thinking innovations, we can design spaces that not only respond to our present needs but also evolve alongside us. The homes, workplaces, and cities of tomorrow will reflect this deeper understanding of how built environments influence behavior, well-being, and connection, ensuring that good design continues to be a force for positive transformation.

How a Space Transforms Into a Place
Transforming a space into a place is a profound and complex process. It begins with the fundamental need for connection and meaning. A space is merely a physical environment defined by its boundaries, materials, and function. However, interacting with that space—whether through movement, memory, or emotional experience—takes on more profound significance and meaning. A space becomes a place when it aligns with our needs and values, reflecting our desires for comfort, safety, identity, and belonging.

From a design perspective, this transformation is often driven by the understanding that the built environment must respond to the nuances of human experience. Spaces are not passive; they actively influence how we feel, interact with others, and see ourselves. For example, spaces designed to encourage connection, like open living areas or community spaces, encourage interaction and cooperation. Similarly, spaces intended for introspection or relaxation, like libraries, gardens, or personal rooms, can become sanctuaries of peace, helping us feel grounded and secure.

Designing a space that transforms into a place involves a delicate balance between aesthetic considerations and functionality. A well-designed space incorporates elements that evoke emotional responses, shape behavior, and support social and cultural needs. Light, color, texture, and scale are all elements that interact with the senses and psyche to evoke warmth, tranquility, or excitement.

Moreover, a place gains its significance through design and the lived experiences that unfold within it, with memory playing a critical role in this transformation. Whether briefly or over many years, the places we inhabit become deeply intertwined with our narratives. A kitchen where a family gathers to cook becomes more than just a place to prepare meals—it symbolizes shared time, love, and tradition. A park where friends meet becomes a place of connection, where shared moments of joy, laughter, or even solace contribute to its meaning. These spaces accumulate emotional and psychological layers that bind us to them, transforming them from neutral environments into places that carry personal and collective meaning.

In addition to individual experiences, shared experiences are key to transforming space into place. A public space—a park, square, or plaza—becomes more than just a location on a map when the community uses it for gatherings, celebrations, protests, or casual interactions. These events imbue the space with collective memory, and the space becomes a symbol of identity, social cohesion, or historical significance. For example, a town square might host annual festivals, political speeches, and casual interactions between locals. Over time, this square might gain significance as a representation of the town's character, history, and the community's values.

Notably, the concept of "place" is not static. It evolves, much like the people and cultures that inhabit it. A place may hold different meanings for individuals depending on their experiences, cultural backgrounds, and societal roles. The space that initially feels unfamiliar or unwelcoming may, over time, become a place of familiarity and comfort as a person or a group grows accustomed to it, personalizes it, and imbues it with meaning. Conversely, places that were once familiar and comforting may evolve into something unsettling or unrecognizable as changes occur, whether due to shifting cultural norms, physical alterations, or personal experiences that alter our perceptions.

The idea of place is deeply tied to identity. Our homes, workplaces, and social spaces reflect and influence who we are. For instance, a house represents our personal identity, family dynamics, and individual memories. Through the design of our homes, we express aspects of our identity and values. Our homes, therefore, become places that anchor us in our narratives, helping us define who we are and where we belong.

Beyond the physical design, places offer a sense of belonging and emotional connection. This feeling of belonging is tied to how we interact with the people and communities around us. A place can become an anchor, offering reassurance, stability, and a sense of rootedness. For example, cultural or religious spaces—churches, temples, or community centers—become places where individuals find spiritual comfort, purpose, and connection to a larger community. These places carry shared histories and values and serve as locations for social interaction, personal reflection, and collective expression.

This connection between space and place is also explored in neurodesign, which recognizes that the physical characteristics of a space can influence mood, behavior, and even cognitive abilities. Designing spaces that cater to our sensory and emotional needs can support our overall mental health. Research in this field suggests that spaces designed using the principles of neuropsychology can help foster feelings of calm, creativity, and focus.

Designing with human well-being in mind is at the heart of the idea that space transforms into place. Spaces that promote comfort, connection, and positive emotions are more likely to become places where individuals feel a sense of belonging and attachment. Conversely, uncomfortable or poorly designed spaces may fail to evoke positive emotions, resulting in alienation or discomfort.

Understanding how space transforms into place is essential for creating functional and meaningful environments. Designing spaces that foster connection, comfort, and a sense of belonging is crucial, whether in architecture, interior design, urban planning, or community development.

Ultimately, the transformation from space to place is an ongoing process shaped by both design and the experiences we have within it. Our spaces provide the foundation for interacting with our surroundings, forming relationships, and shaping our sense of identity. By understanding this dynamic, we can create spaces that enhance our physical surroundings and nourish our emotional, psychological, and social needs while supporting our growth, healing, and connection to something greater than ourselves.

PART II
What Psychology Teaches Us About Harmonious Living

Home as a Mirror of Self

Our homes are far more than four walls and a roof—they are mirrors of our identities, values, and relationships. How we design and interact with our living spaces reflects who we are, what we prioritize, and how we connect with those who share our space. Whether it's through cherished mementos, colors that evoke comfort, or the arrangement of furniture that fosters togetherness, our homes tell a story about us and the life we want to create.

A Reflection of Identity and Connection

The home is an intimate portrait of the self that we shape by our tastes, routines, and the dynamics we share with others. A minimalist, clutter-free space might reflect a desire for simplicity and clarity, while a home filled with books and art could symbolize curiosity and a love for learning. For cohabitants, how those spaces are shared—whether through collaborative designs or individualized areas—reflects the balance between unity and independence within their relationship.

Beyond aesthetics, how we use space reveals deeper personal and psychological insights. For example, people who constantly rearrange the furniture and update the décor may indicate a personality that thrives on change and adaptability. Conversely, people who leave their homes largely unchanged for years might suggest a need for stability and nostalgia. Understanding these patterns can offer insight into how we navigate change, relationships, and personal growth within our domestic environments.

Some homes vividly reflect personal histories and dreams. When someone steps into a home, they can often feel the essence of the person who inhabits it—their personality, passions, and experiences are woven into the décor, colors, and even the way furniture is arranged. A musician's home may have instruments scattered throughout, a piano in the living room, and shelves lined with CDs, reinforcing a connection to sound and creativity. A couple passionate about travel might have a gallery wall of framed tickets, maps, postcards, and photos taken of them in front of famous landmarks, reminding them of their shared adventures and their longing for exploration. A great-grandmother who cherishes her heritage might fill her home with heirlooms, embroidered textiles, and antique furniture passed down for generations, ensuring that her family's cultural legacy stays alive.

Approaching Spaces with Intention and Meaning

When we approach our homes with intention, they become more than functional spaces; they become environments imbued with meaning and purpose. Intentional design asks us to consider what we need and how we want to feel in our spaces. Do we want a bedroom that supports deep rest? A kitchen that encourages family bonding? A home office that sparks creativity? By aligning the design of our spaces with our goals and values, we ensure that every element contributes to a meaningful, supportive environment.

Intention also extends to how we interact with our spaces daily. Rituals, such as lighting a candle before meditation, playing soft music in the morning, or setting out flowers on a dining table, create layers of emotional connection between us and our homes. These small acts contribute to a sense of mindfulness, reminding us to engage fully with our environment and reinforce the emotions we wish to cultivate within it.

Some homeowners even craft spaces to serve as vision boards for their futures. A writer might create a cozy nook filled with inspirational books and a vintage desk to enhance focus and imagination. A fitness enthusiast may transform a corner of the home into a wellness sanctuary with yoga mats, essential oils, and an open window to let in the morning light. Every design choice, conscious or subconscious, creates an environment that either nurtures or hinders personal growth.

Additionally, the way we design our homes can reflect the cultural traditions and familial legacies that shape our identity. A home filled with heirlooms, traditional motifs in furniture and textiles, or handmade crafts passed down through generations speaks to a deep respect for ancestry and heritage. Designating a space for religious or spiritual practice or intentionally placing art that speaks to one's background further strengthens the cultural bond between home and self. Weaving elements of our cultural and familial history into our living spaces creates an environment that honors our past and reinforces our sense of belonging and identity.

Homes as Sanctuaries for Well-Being

Our homes can nurture emotional, physical, and spiritual well-being. Emotionally, homes offer a sense of safety and belonging, where we can process our feelings and recharge. Physically, thoughtful layouts and ergonomic designs support our health, promoting movement, comfort, and rest. Spiritually, intentional spaces like meditation corners, reading nooks, or gardens create opportunities for reflection and connection with something greater than us.

In recent years, research has highlighted environmental design's impact on stress reduction and overall happiness. Studies suggest that incorporating elements of nature into home spaces, like houseplants, natural materials, and water features, can lower cortisol levels and improve mood. Additionally, an organized and clean home can directly influence an individual's mental clarity and lead to inner peace and balance (Yin et al. 2018).

The way we create personal sanctuaries within our homes also reflects our self-care habits and emotional needs. A window seat filled with books, soft pillows, and natural light signals a love for solitude and intellectual retreat, while a music corner filled with instruments suggests a need for musical expression. When we design spaces that align with our wellness practices, they support our growth, restoration, and joy.

For some, their homes become healing spaces. A cancer survivor might fill their space with soft textiles, soothing colors, and calming scents to create a restorative environment. A person recovering from grief might design a memorial space with cherished photos and candles as a quiet place to reflect on their lost loved one. By designing homes with well-being in mind, we ensure that they not only shelter us but also support our emotional and spiritual health.

Creating Your Mirror of Self

You can transform your home into a true reflection of your identity by starting with small, intentional steps: Declutter spaces to reveal what matters most. Add elements that resonate with your personality and bring you joy, like art, textures, or scents. Collaborate with your cohabitants to design shared spaces that honor your connections while carving out areas you can call your own. Your home is a living, breathing extension of you—an environment where your identity, relationships, and well-being come together. By approaching it with intention and care, you can create a space that reflects who you are and supports who you want to become.

As we evolve, our homes need to evolve with us. Life transitions, such as a career shift, a growing family, or personal development, can prompt modifications to our living spaces. By reassessing and adapting our home environments, we can ensure that they continue to support our well-being and aspirations. Ultimately, creating a home that mirrors the self is not about perfection but about creating a space where authenticity, connection, and personal fulfillment can thrive.

By recognizing that our homes are living representations of our dreams, relationships, and cultural influences, we gain a deeper appreciation for the power of design in shaping our lives. The most meaningful spaces are not those curated for perfection but those that embrace the unique, evolving nature of the people who inhabit them. When we craft a home that reflects our true selves, we create an environment where we can fully thrive, heal, and grow.

5

Foundational Psychological Models of Neurodesign

Understanding human psychology is essential for creating living environments that support emotional, mental, and physical well-being. It is not just about the spaces themselves but about the psychological effects those spaces have on us. By understanding the psychological models that influence human behavior and emotional responses, we can design environments that stimulate mental clarity, emotional health, and personal growth.

The psychological models that we will explore—Maslow's hierarchy of needs, attachment theory, mindfulness, developmental psychology, and other theories—will help inform our understanding of human experience within a space and their practical applications in neurodesign. Each of these models provides insight into how we interact with our environments and how those environments can either support or hinder our emotional and psychological needs. For instance, Maslow's hierarchy of needs shows us how our homes can meet fundamental needs like safety, belonging, and self-actualization. Attachment theory helps us understand the importance of creating spaces that provide emotional security. Mindfulness encourages us to create environments that promote presence and emotional regulation, while developmental psychology allows us to consider how our needs evolve as we age.

Recognizing how these models address human behavior and emotional responses will provide a deeper appreciation for how design choices directly impact mood, well-being, and overall health.

Environmental Psychology: The Relationship Between Us and Our Environment

MASLOW'S HIERARCHY OF NEEDS

Abraham Maslow's original five-stage model is a popular hierarchical guide covering basic developmental needs that motivate people's behavior. Modern interpretations view it less as a hierarchy and more as motivated needs to be satisfied at any point. The model was expanded in the 1970s to include three additional levels: cognitive, aesthetic, and transcendence needs (see Figure 5.1). The expanded model consists of the following:

1. *Biological and physiological needs:* air, food, drink, shelter, warmth, sex, and sleep
2. *Safety needs:* protection from elements, security, order, law, stability, freedom
3. *Love and belongingness needs:* friendship, intimacy, trust, acceptance, receiving and giving affection and love, affiliating, being part of a group (e.g., family, friends, coworkers)

4. *Esteem needs*: esteem for oneself (e.g., dignity, achievement, mastery, independence) and the desire for recognition or respect from others (e.g., status, prestige)
5. *Cognitive needs:* knowledge and understanding, curiosity, exploration, meaning, predictability
6. *Aesthetic needs:* appreciation and search for beauty, balance, and form
7. *Self-actualization needs:* realizing personal potential, self-fulfillment, seeking personal growth and peak experiences
8. *Transcendence needs*: values that transcend beyond the personal self (e.g., mystical experiences, experiences with nature, aesthetic experiences, sexual experiences, service to others, the pursuit of science, religious faith)

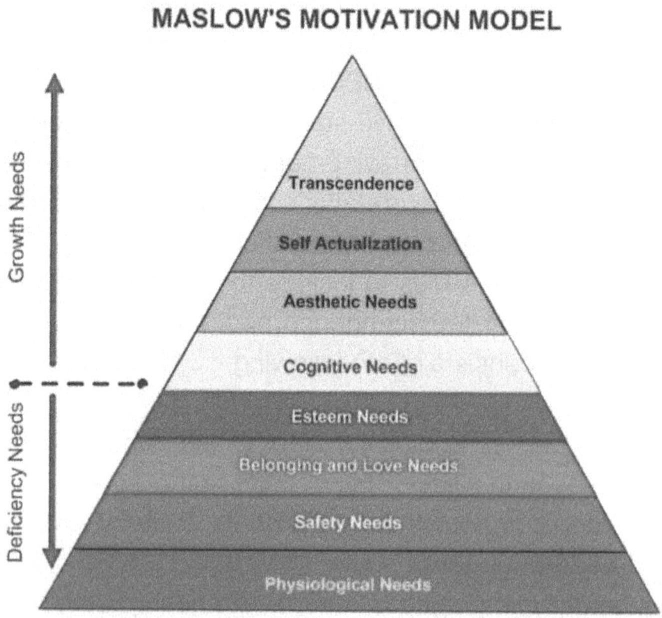

Figure 5.1. Maslow's expanded hierarchy of needs. *Source:* Maslow 1954.

Harmonious living, for our purposes, is informed by the updated eight-stage model, which includes not only basic deficiency needs but also cognitive needs (promoting curiosity in our inner and outer worlds), aesthetic needs (appreciating beauty and seeking balance and nature), self-actualization needs (creating aesthetic experiences in enlivened spaces), and even transcendence needs.

Several psychological models address the concept of belonging and its impact on mental health, relationships, and overall well-being. Their approaches explore how human connection and a sense of community influence behavior, emotions, and cognitive processes. The following are some of the primary psychological frameworks that highlight the importance of belonging:

1. Humanistic Psychology
Humanistic psychology places a strong emphasis on the intrinsic need for connection and belonging as part of personal growth.

- **Maslow's Hierarchy of Needs**: Maslow (1970) identified belongingness as a foundational human need, situated just above basic physiological and safety needs. He argued that social connection, love, and acceptance are essential for individuals to achieve self-actualization and reach their full potential.
- **Rogers' Person-Centered Therapy**: Rogers (1980) believed that belonging and unconditional positive regard are critical for personal growth. He emphasized the importance of supportive relationships in developing self-esteem and authentic self-expression.

2. Social Psychology
Social psychology extensively studies how belonging influences behavior and emotions within the context of group dynamics.

- **Tajfel and Turner's Social Identity Theory**: (Tajfel and Turner 1979) This theory explores how belonging to a group shapes self-concept and behavior. It highlights the role of group memberships (e.g., cultural, social, or familial) in creating a sense of identity and connection.
- **Baumeister and Leary's Belongingness Hypothesis**: Baumeister and Leary (1995) proposed that the need to belong is a fundamental human motivation and that a lack of belonging leads to significant psychological distress, including loneliness and depression.

3. Attachment Theory

Developed by Bowlby (1969) and expanded by Ainsworth (1979), attachment theory underscores the role that early relationships play in fostering a sense of safety and belonging.

- Secure attachment in childhood, formed through consistent and loving caregiving, provides the foundation for healthy relationships and a strong sense of belonging in adulthood.
- This theory also explores how disruptions in attachment can lead to difficulties in forming meaningful connections and a sense of isolation.

4. Positive Psychology

Positive psychology addresses the role of belonging in achieving happiness and well-being.

- **Martin Seligman's PERMA Model**: Seligman's (2011) framework for well-being includes "relationships" as a core element. His model highlights how belonging and social bonds contribute to life satisfaction and resilience.
- Studies in positive psychology show that nurturing social connections leads to greater levels of happiness, health, and productivity.

HUMANISTIC PSYCHOLOGY

Harmonious living draws from the premise of Carl Rogers's "humanistic psychology," which is based on the assumptions that humans have free will, are inherently good, creative, and unique, and are intrinsically motivated to self-actualize (Rogers 2013). In practice, humanistic psychology advocates for unconditional love and positive regard for humans, supporting our authenticity and capacity for growth. How we regard ourselves can mirror how we regard our spaces and reflect our inner desires in design preferences while supporting a natural curiosity to grow in our homes. The selection and placement of art, for example, can reflect our true selves, and our homes hopefully can support this authentic expression. In design, if we need to feel more comfortable growing ourselves, maybe consider, for example, an opening to a garden that allows us to freely navigate between our inner and outer worlds.

ERIKSON'S STAGES OF DEVELOPMENT

As with Maslow's hierarchy of needs, which helps determine what motivates and inspires us in our living spaces, the next crucial psychological model to highlight is Erik Erikson's stages of development, which, like in Maslow's hierarchy, are no longer seen as necessarily linear but suggestive of mastery at any point in our lives. While they may never be completed, they are conflicts to resolve (see Table 5.1). Erik Erikson's stages of development outline key psychological challenges at various stages of life. As you can see outlined in the table, trust is formed in infancy, while toddlers balance independence with doubt. Children explore and build competence but may feel inferior if they fail. Adolescents seek their identity, and young adults focus on forming relationships. In middle adulthood, individuals strive to contribute to society, and in late adulthood, they reflect on their lives with either integrity or regret. Each stage builds on the previous, guiding emotional growth. In harmonious living, we see these stages as mindsets and characteristics to develop as we design our homes and each room, emphasizing individual growth while evolving our relationships. For example, we can keep these stages in mind as we support a child's play in their room by watching what they play with and how they move around the space and as we support in-laws in an ADU—by giving back and supporting each other in our homes and lives—generativity. The "intimacy versus isolation" stage can be identified by creating spaces to commune and connect while not isolating and hiding.

Table 5.1. Erikson's Stages of Development

Stage	Psychosocial Crisis	Basic Virtue	Age
1.	Trust vs. Mistrust	Hope	0-1½
2.	Autonomy vs. Shame	Will	1½-3
3.	Initiative vs. Guilt	Purpose	3-5
4.	Industry vs. Inferiority	Competency	5-12
5.	Identity vs. Role Confusion	Fidelity	12-18
6.	Intimacy vs. Isolation	Love	18-40
7.	Generativity vs. Stagnation	Care	40-65
8.	Ego Integrity vs. Despair	Wisdom	65+

Source: Erickson 1950.

ATTACHMENT THEORY

A central tenet to how we form secure and thriving relationships is based on John Bowlby's attachment theory. According to attachment theory, securely functioning relationships stem from our earlier parental relationships in which, back in infancy, we explored the world from a secure base. Parenting is provided not necessarily by a biological parent but by a central support figure who offers reliable and safe feedback and reassures us that we are seen and that our primal needs of hunger and emotions are met. This support figure alleges to give us the inner blueprint that we need to safely explore our world, knowing that we then have our own secure base to go back to. You could call this our own centering, but it is our integration of knowing we can rely on ourselves just like we could with a parental figure.

Attachment theory gave way to the concept of "attunement" and how we can attune to ourselves, our relationships, and, importantly, our spaces. The more attuned we are to our needs, wants, and desires, the more we can be attuned to others. For example, if I am attuned to my morning coffee ritual as a need to get going in my day, maybe my partner will attune to this as well and lovingly start the coffee.

Attunement then can be applied to how one attunes their spaces to meet their living needs. The placement of my furniture and lighting in my office, for example, attunes to my need for a cozy start in the morning, where I sit on my analyst lounge couch with a beanbag ottoman, low lighting from a lamp, and my charged coffee mug. My space reflects my inner needs for morning rituals and supports my intentional goal of getting my day going. Attunement can further be seen as a regulatory mechanism for adjusting to our needs, desires, and moods. Our relationships and our homes reflect us and serve as regulations. How we employ a home or space to secure functionality while promoting curiosity and exploration is the key to "Artful Living."

SOMATIC MODELS

The next model to highlight is the somatic psychological model. We know and feel attunement via the body as our appraisal system. This system holds information on a primitive level, such as in fight-or-flight or when we feel a sense of awe in front of a painting or on a hike. Our bodies are our truest felt-sense barometers and can be trusted appraisal systems.

Sensory Integration in Design
The integration of sensory variables in a home environment can be experienced in a spectrum of sensory sensitivities, including sight, sound, smell, taste, touch, vestibular (sense of motion in the body), and proprioceptive (sense of the position of the body). While sensory integration modalities are commonly based in occupational therapy and have shown benefits in regulating individuals diagnosed with more hypo- or hypersensitivities on the autism spectrum, integrating the sensory system can be applied to a wide range of sensory sensitivities. Using a lighter paint color palette, softer rugs, temperature controls for showers, and visual cues to alert visitors are all examples of design solutions to keep in mind for hyper-aroused sensitivities.

The Embodied Space
Applying design psychology to healing is based on principles of trauma recovery that work with our primitive navigational and emotional systems. Levine and Frederick (1997) demonstrate how somatic experiencing, when paired with design principles, can influence living environments by deepening the connection between the body and space. Levine and Frederick introduce the concept of the "felt sense," which involves the arousal system, including both the sympathetic and parasympathetic nervous systems, and the reptilian brain, which governs fight, flight, freeze, and dissociation responses. These highly aroused responses, as well as intense emotions such as rage and panic, are often associated with trauma, but this is not all bad. Because by cultivating awareness of the body and using this "felt sense" as a guide, we can safely experience these survival responses and discharge them. The body acts as the gatekeeper to these processes, and we can use its natural techniques, such as tracking and orienting, to become more present in our surroundings and pendulation to regulate the body into states of calm. We can

also discharge trauma through physical sensations like shaking, tingling, or heat.

Another method applied is found in decoupling—the separation of embodied memories and environmental associations. This method enables individuals to create new meanings in their physical spaces. Also, using imagery can unlock unconscious memories stored in the body, allowing for a deeper connection between the environment and personal healing.

COUPLES AND FAMILY SYSTEMS MODELS
The following models describe of how relational cues identified in couples therapy can facilitate healing through activation systems and relational intervention. Couples therapist and researcher Harville Hendrix (1990) has identified a model of therapy called Imago therapy, which describes the couples as having individual inner wounds, usually based in childhood trauma, that can be activated and aroused within the relational system. Hendrix surmised that the unconscious attractions we have with our partners are part of a need for the corrective experience from our childhood relational wounds and that the relationship serves to heal these earlier wounds (Hendrix 1990).

Therapy models found in attachment similarly aim to rewire the individual's activation through the relational system. Stan Tatkin surmised that our activation body responses, much like somatic experiencing, can be healed through the relationship. For instance, early childhood wounds triggered by interpreting a facial expression as disapproving can be corrected by the relational reassurance that one's partner is affirming. Applications of design psychology principles, as corroborated with the Imago and attachment models of therapy, can inform the design environment as its bidirectional relational partner (Tatkin 2011). Much like attachment interventions, individual therapy and couples therapy can inform a bidirectional relationship between the person and the environment.

Also, family systems psychological models based upon Salvador Minuchin's structural family systems theory state that families tend toward homeostasis. How do we implement design supports and guidance that encourage healthy growth and change as a system, and how is it reflected in the living space? Furthermore, Bowen's family systems theory speaks to the need for individuation and differentiation from the family system toward individual growth, as seen in an adolescent. This involves creating a space that encourages personal expression and increases socialization opportunities with peers.

Some applications of design principles for harmonious relationships include:

- She shed/man cave: Individuation promoted through separate creative spaces while living together as a couple
- Negotiation: Integrating a couple's design style
- Imago: Assessing each partner's wounds to promote healing through spatial needs of intimacy and separation
- Attunement: Building secure attachment through gauging traumatic activation responses. For example, separate bathrooms can diffuse conflict

JUNGIAN ANALYTICAL PSYCHOLOGY

The contributions of psychoanalyst Carl Jung, who gave birth to philosophies on the mythical and symbolic in dream and active life, explain Jung's concepts of alchemy as a transcendent nature of the human psyche can be seen in the home's objects, furniture, art, and architectural designs (Jung 1968). The alchemical process is seen in image and symbolism, unlocking the magic. The image and symbolism of each room and its historical and symbolic meaning can be found in Ronnberg's (2010) *The Book of Symbols: Reflections on Archetypal Images*. For example, the book talks about the bedroom as a place to fulfill the need for rest or sex and intimacy, and we design our spaces to reflect these needs, wants, and desires. Jung further speaks to the archetypal that are stored in our collective unconscious, such as the themes of mother, father, and snakes. They are encoded in our evolution and are activated in our present bodies and spaces, such as when we sense an intruder and need safety, and support our design to navigate for these symbolic cues. Artwork can hold symbols and archetypes of lineage, time, and feelings and can be transformative in their place in our spaces. Jungian concepts of Anima (feminine) and Animus (masculine) balance all of us individually and collectively in our spaces (Jung 1968). Feminine ideals of warmth, connection, and beauty can be highlighted in a bathroom spa designed for respite, while office space uses a more masculine energy of productivity.

STRENGTH-BASED MODELS
Narrative and solution-focused therapy are briefly mentioned here as they are strength-based models that formed the basis of my clinical social work education. Narrative therapy, pioneered by Michael White and David Epston, externalized the problem from the individual while empowering them to create their own story (Epston and Marsten 2016). In solution-focused therapy, the solution is focused upon more than the problem and becomes a practical and goal-oriented approach to problem-solving—a can-do mentality. Design choices are intentional and creative, acknowledging that complexities in design challenges will reliably arise. Finally, Martin Seligman's "Positive Psychology" (PERMA; Seligman 2012) purports the following five elements, both eudemonic (virtues of well-being) and hedonic (enjoyment and pleasure), contribute to well-being:

- Positive emotion
- Engagement
- Relationships
- Meaning
- Achievement

MINDFULNESS

Based on Eastern philosophies such as Buddhism, mindfulness now plays a significant role in well-being and health. Mindfulness as a tool and practice reminds us to stay present with ourselves and our spaces, thereby lowering stress and expanding contentment and joy in our lives. When we are mindful, we take in our surroundings without judgment and act with curiosity. We are alert, active, awake to our surroundings, and fully embodied in our senses. It serves to allow and grow versus defining and instructing. When we are mindful in our selection of our architectural and interior design elements, we can also envision our spaces to their fullest potential. Openness gives way to curiosity, which manifests the vision of a dream space. Mindfulness is intentional and, therefore, conscious and holds a connection to our everyday design objects, thus enlivening our homes and our surroundings. One could say it is an energetic thing, like you just know how you feel in a space you love. As we often say, "It just has a great vibe." Is this vibe the energy that reverberates from all the love and intention in the design of that home? Does it feel grounded and rooted because of those original hardwood floors from the 1920s that exude history? We save a family heirloom because it roots us to lineage, and we care for it in a way that allows it to shine and continue to live on in our hearts and homes. How we set our table, replete with elements to entertain and socialize, creates a meaningful space of connection.

6

What is Harmonious Living? The Relationship Factor

A well-balanced design can strengthen relationships and enhance the personal well-being of everyone within the household. How we interact and connect in our environment significantly influences stress levels and overall health. In this chapter, we will highlight the importance of the following tenets of harmonious living:

- Embodying and enlivening our spaces so that they support every aspect of our lives and the lives of those who live with us
- Supporting relationship dynamics in the home
- How our home affects and influences coregulation with our cohabitants
- Designing homes that can transform ourselves and our relationships

- Creating intentional, mindful, and purposeful places of higher well-being
- Negotiating design decisions
- Communication dynamics in building or remodeling a new home
- Applying design strategies to spaces to support singles, couples, and families

House of Relationship: Jenna and Tom

When Jenna and Tom bought their first house together, they were excited. It was everything they had dreamed of—a cozy two-bedroom with lots of natural light and a big backyard for their dog, Milo. But as they settled in, cracks began to appear—not in the walls, but in their relationship.

The kitchen felt too cramped for two people to cook in simultaneously, and they bickered over who should take the lead. Jenna preferred quiet evenings reading in the living room, but Tom often wanted to watch sports, leaving one feeling displaced. Their bedroom, with its harsh lighting and cluttered corners, became more of a storage room than a sanctuary for rest. Slowly, the tension built. They started avoiding conversations, snapping at each other over small things, and retreating into their own worlds.

One evening, after a particularly heated argument about who left the laundry on the floor, Jenna sat on the couch and said, "I don't think it's just us. I think this house, our space, isn't working for us." Tom agreed and started investigating ways to make their home feel more supportive. Through his research, they discovered the concept of harmonious living—that well-balanced design can have a positive impact on relationships and enhance personal well-being.

The Transformation Begins

Jenna and Tom worked together to reevaluate how their space could reflect their relationship instead of working against it. They started with the kitchen. A designer suggested creating designated zones—one for meal prep and another for cooking—so they could work together without stepping on each other's toes. They installed under-cabinet lighting and hung a chalkboard on the wall where they could leave notes for each other, turning a space of tension into one of collaboration.

In the living room, they found a compromise by arranging the furniture to create two zones: a comfortable reading nook for Jenna and a separate area for Tom's TV. A bookshelf filled with books, games, and mementos that reflected their shared interests connected the two spaces.

The bedroom became their sanctuary. They chose a calming pale green paint color, added blackout curtains that enhanced their sleep, and removed clutter, replacing it with a few meaningful items—a framed photo from their wedding, a small vase of fresh flowers, and a journal they started keeping together to jot down things they appreciated about each other.

The Impact of Harmonious Design

As their physical space transformed, so did their relationship. The kitchen became a place where they laughed and cooked together, each in their zone but working toward a shared goal. The living room, no longer a battleground of competing interests, became a space where they could coexist, each enjoying their hobbies while still feeling connected. The bedroom became a retreat where they could relax and reconnect after long days.

What surprised Jenna and Tom most was how these changes affected their stress levels. Their arguments became less and less heated, and they started spending more quality time together, not because they had to but because they wanted to. For Jenna and Tom, harmonious living was not just about fixing their house—it was about building a life together that felt aligned, supportive, and filled with joy. And that's the true power of a well-balanced space.

The Relationship Factor in Harmonious Living

Jenna and Tom's story illustrates how much our living environment influences how we connect and interact. When our homes are designed with intention—balancing individual needs with shared spaces—they foster relationships that thrive. Harmonious living is not just about aesthetics or organization; it's about creating a space that strengthens the emotional, physical, and relational well-being of everyone in the household.

The Psychology of Relationship

In my experience working as a clinician, I have found four main theories to be the most useful models for how we can live harmoniously in relationships, in families, and with our peers: the Gottman Method, Imago Relationship Therapy (IRT), Bowen family systems theory, and Minuchin's structural family therapy. I believe harmony begins when we can support positive communication based on Gottman's principles (1999). For example, we might avoid Gottman's "four horsemen"—criticism, condemnations, control, and stonewalling—and strive toward his seven principles for successful marriages: build love maps to understand each other deeply; nurture fondness and admiration; turn toward each other in small, everyday moments; allow mutual influence; solve solvable problems; manage conflict while accepting differences; and create shared meaning within the relationship. Imago therapy, developed by Hendrix and Hunt (2007), works with our deeper inner wounds as a precursor to how we can heal in relationships. Bowen (2017) spoke about the individuation process in our self-development as we differentiate from the old ways of functioning in our family of origin. Finally, Minuchin (2021) worked within the family system to identify how we triangulate others into dynamics and our tendency toward the status quo. I have applied all these theories to how we can grow ourselves and our relationships while designing our spaces and functioning in our homes.

Relationship Models: Building Stronger Connections at Home

Your home is not just a place where you live—it is the backdrop for your relationships. Whether it is with your partner, your kids, or your extended family, how you connect with the people you share your space with plays a huge role in how happy and healthy your home feels. Over the years, researchers and therapists have developed powerful models to help us better understand and improve these connections. Let's break down four popular approaches that are designed to strengthen relationships and create harmony in your home.

1. Gottman Method of Couples Therapy: The Science of Love

The **Gottman Method**, developed by Drs. John and Julie Gottman (2024), is based on decades of research into what makes relationships succeed or fail. At its core, this method focuses on building a strong foundation of friendship, managing conflict effectively, and creating shared meaning in a relationship.

Key takeaways to apply to your relationship:

- **Turn toward, not away:** Small moments matter. Pay attention to your partner's needs and show you care, even with the little things, like responding to a smile or a question.
- **Master conflict:** The goal is not to avoid disagreements but to handle them with respect and curiosity. Learn to listen and validate your partner's feelings, even when you disagree.
- **Build shared meaning:** Create rituals, shared goals, and values that bring you closer as a team.

2. Harville Hendrix Imago Therapy: Healing Through Connection

Developed by Hendrix and Hunt (2008), **Imago therapy** helps couples understand how their past influences their present relationships.

This method views conflicts as opportunities for growth and encourages partners to work together to heal old wounds while developing a deeper bond.

Key takeaways for your relationship:

- **Your partner as your mirror:** Many current conflicts stem from unmet needs or wounds from your past. Recognizing this can help you approach disagreements with empathy and understanding.
- **Intentional dialogue:** Practice active listening by mirroring your partner's words, validating their feelings, and sharing your perspective without judgment.
- **Focus on connection:** Shift your energy from blame to curiosity, asking, "How can we grow from this together?"

3. Minuchin Family Systems: The Family as a Whole

Minuchin's family systems therapy, created by Salvador Minuchin (2021), views the family as a dynamic system where every member affects the others. Instead of focusing on one person's problem, this approach looks at how patterns and structures within the family contribute to challenges.

Key takeaways for your family:

- **Boundaries matter:** Healthy families have clear but flexible boundaries. For example, parents should have authority, but children should also feel heard and respected.
- **Patterns over individuals:** Instead of blaming one person for a problem, look at how family interactions might be reinforcing unhealthy dynamics.
- **Small shifts, big changes:** Adjusting how you communicate or set boundaries can ripple through the whole family, improving relationships and reducing tension.

4. Bowen Family Systems Theory: Balancing Emotion and Logic

Developed by Murray Bowen (2017), the **Bowen family systems theory** focuses on how families influence individual behavior. Bowen believed that family dynamics are passed down through generations and that balancing emotional closeness and independence is key to healthy relationships.

Key takeaways for your family:

- **Differentiate yourself:** Healthy families support individuality. Maintain your sense of self while staying connected to your loved ones.
- **Emotional triangles:** Be mindful of "triangles," where a third person is drawn into a conflict between two others. This dynamic can create tension, so focus on resolving issues directly with the person involved.
- **Generational patterns:** Reflect on how family behaviors and beliefs have been passed down and consider how they shape your choices and interactions.

Bringing These Models into Your Home

You do not need to be a therapist to apply these ideas to your life. Start by reflecting on your relationships and family dynamics:

- Do you validate your partner's feelings and turn toward them during challenging moments, as the Gottman Method (1999) suggests?
- Are you curious about how your past influences your conflicts, as Imago therapy (2008) encourages?
- Are your family's boundaries clear and respectful, following Minuchin's (2021) principles?

- Can you maintain your individuality while staying connected, as Bowen (2017) advises?

By incorporating these strategies, you can create a home that is not just functional but a place where relationships flourish, connection deepens, and everyone feels valued.

Relationship Transformational Story: Laura and Mike

Laura and Mike were thrilled when they bought their dream home. It was a charming, sunlit space with a backyard perfect for their kids, Emily and Jack, and their dog, Max. But as they settled into the house, their initial excitement shifted to frustration. The cramped kitchen became a battleground over cooking duties. The living room was so cluttered with toys and mismatched furniture, it felt chaotic and uninviting. Their bedroom, filled with laundry and harsh lighting, offered little respite from their growing frustrations. Over time, their communication frayed, and instead of being a sanctuary, the house became a source of conflict.

Feeling disconnected and overwhelmed, Laura and Mike turned to a couples therapist for guidance. Through therapy, they discovered how the design and function of their home played a significant role in their relationship dynamics. By applying relationship-building skills from the four major theories of couples therapy alongside neurodesign concepts, they began transforming their space and connection.

Applying Couples Therapy to Harmonious Living

1. Gottman Method: Strengthening the Foundation of Love

Their therapist introduced them to the **Gottman Method (1999)**, which focuses on building a solid foundation of friendship, managing conflict, and creating shared meaning. Laura and Mike realized their home lacked spaces for positive interaction. So they reimagined their kitchen as a place of collaboration. With the help of a designer, they created designated zones: one for meal prep and another for cooking. They also used the refrigerator door as a place to leave notes of appreciation, like "Thank you for dinner last night" or "Good luck with your meeting today." These small, intentional acts of gratitude rekindled feelings of connection and partnership.

2. Harville Hendrix's Imago Therapy: Healing Through Understanding

Through Imago therapy, Laura and Mike learned that their arguments often stemmed from unresolved wounds and unmet needs from their past. For instance, Laura realized her frustration with the disorganized living room mirrored the feelings of chaos she experienced in her childhood home, while Mike's tendency to avoid those conversations stemmed from a fear of criticism. Armed with this understanding, they approached their living room redesign with empathy. Using Marie Kondo's system of organizing by categories, they got rid of stuff together and kept items that sparked joy for them, like family photos and books (Kondo 2016). They created a cozy reading space for Laura and a designated play area for the kids, ensuring the space felt welcoming and balanced.

3. Minuchin Family Systems: Establishing Healthy Boundaries

Their therapist also introduced them to **Minuchin's** (2021) **family systems theory**, which emphasizes clear, flexible boundaries. The bedroom, which used to be cluttered with work laptops and laundry, became a sanctuary for their relationship. They removed all work-related items, painted the walls a calming shade of blue, and added dimmable lamps for soft lighting. A "no screens after 9 p.m." rule ensured they could focus on each other without distractions, which made the space more intimate and inviting.

4. Bowen Family Systems: Balancing Connection and Independence

Finally, **Bowen** (2017) **family systems theory** taught Laura and Mike the importance of balancing individuality and togetherness. They carved out personal spaces within the home where they could recharge independently. Laura took over a corner of the bedroom and turned it into a meditation area with soft cushions, candles, and a small indoor fountain. Mike repurposed part of the basement for his woodworking projects. These personal retreats gave them the freedom to nurture their individuality while strengthening their connection in shared areas.

The Transformation of Their Home and Relationship

As they made these changes, Laura and Mike noticed profound shifts in their relationship. The kitchen became a space of teamwork and laughter, the living room a cozy retreat for family time, and the bedroom a haven for intimacy and rest. The backyard became a shared project where the family planted a garden together, incorporating elements of biophilic design. They added flowers for beauty, vegetables for nourishment, and a water feature to bring the soothing sounds of nature into their space. Research shows that natural elements can reduce cortisol levels and enhance well-being, and the family felt those benefits immediately. Their communication improved as they applied the skills they learned in therapy, like active listening and validation. Arguments became less frequent and less intense, replaced by curiosity and compassion. Most importantly, their home began to reflect their shared values of love, respect, and growth.

The Relationship Factor in Harmonious Living

Laura and Mike's story illustrates how the intersection of thoughtful design and relationship-building skills can transform both a home and the people who live in it. By integrating principles from couples therapy with intentional design, they created an environment that not only reduced stress but also deepened their connection. Harmonious living is not just about beautiful spaces; it is about fostering relationships, reducing tension, and creating a home that supports everyone's well-being. For Laura and Mike, their home became more than a place to live—it became a sanctuary where they thrived.

Healthy Home/Healthy Relationships

A healthy home is more than a well-designed or organized space—it is an environment that nurtures connection, reduces stress, and supports the emotional and physical well-being of its inhabitants. When our living spaces are intentionally designed to promote comfort, communication, and collaboration, they become powerful tools for building healthy relationships.

1. A Home that Reduces Stress Improves Interactions
Research shows that cluttered, chaotic spaces lead to higher stress levels and more frequent conflicts. But a well-maintained, thoughtfully arranged home can have the opposite effect, creating a sense of calm that helps inhabitants manage life's challenges with greater patience. A functional kitchen, for example, can turn mealtime into a shared, enjoyable experience rather than a source of frustration.

2. Intentional Design Promotes Communication
The layout and functionality of a home directly impact how people interact. Open floor plans encourage conversation and togetherness, while designated private spaces allow for moments of solitude and reflection. A living room arranged with circular seating, for

instance, encourages eye contact and makes it easier to connect, while shared projects like creating a family garden or decorating a space together can strengthen bonds through teamwork.

3. Personal Space Supports Individual Well-Being
Healthy relationships require a balance of independence and togetherness, and a well-designed home provides both. When each person has a space to recharge—whether it is a quiet reading space, a home office, or a meditation corner—they are better equipped to show up as their best self in shared interactions. This balance reduces the likelihood of conflict and ensures everyone's needs are respected.

4. A Sanctuary for Rest and Renewal
Bedrooms, in particular, play a crucial role in maintaining healthy relationships. A clutter-free, calming bedroom featuring soothing colors and comfortable bedding inspires better sleep, which directly impacts mood and emotional regulation. Couples who prioritize their bedroom as a sanctuary for rest and intimacy are more likely to experience deeper connection and lower stress.

5. Shared Spaces Foster Togetherness and Belonging
Spaces like dining rooms, outdoor patios, and family rooms create opportunities for shared experiences, which are the building blocks of strong relationships. Regular rituals, such as family dinners, movie nights, or gardening together, reinforce a sense of belonging and help people feel more connected.

6. A Reflection of Shared Values
A healthy home reflects the values and aspirations of the people who live in it. When a couple or family works together to create a space that aligns with their goals—whether through art, design, or shared

projects—they strengthen their sense of unity. A home that tells the story of its inhabitants becomes a source of pride and a reminder of what they have built together.

Harmonizing the Home: Coregulation Is Cohabitation
When designed intentionally, a home becomes an ally in cultivating healthy relationships. It reduces stress, enhances communication, and fosters meaningful connections, creating a foundation where love and trust can flourish. A healthy home is not just about where we live—it's also about how we live together. Coregulation and cohabitation are foundational to creating a harmonious home and thriving relationships. Coregulation is how individuals help each other manage their emotions and stress through connection, empathy, and shared calming behaviors. For example, a soothing tone of voice, a warm hug, or even simply being present during stressful times can help partners or family members feel grounded and supported. Cohabitation, on the other hand, emphasizes the art of living together in a shared space, balancing individual needs with the collective dynamic. A home that facilitates coregulation and cohabitation fosters an environment where emotional safety and mutual respect can thrive. Intentional design can play a critical role—spaces that encourage connection, such as open living areas or shared dining spaces, help nurture coregulation. At the same time, personal retreats provide the independence needed for healthy cohabitation. These practices create a supportive atmosphere where relationships deepen, conflicts are diffused, and everyone feels seen, valued, and at peace.

The Power of Belonging: Why It Matters for Our Well-Being
Belonging is one of our most fundamental psychological needs. Rooted in our evolutionary history, being part of a group or community provides emotional security, reduces stress, and builds

resilience. When we feel like we belong—whether in our families, friendships, or communities—we experience a sense of grounding that directly supports our mental and physical health. Research consistently shows that strong social connections can lower cortisol levels, improve immune function, and even increase longevity.

Conversely, a lack of belonging can be deeply damaging. Loneliness and exclusion are linked to anxiety, depression, and a heightened risk of chronic health issues. Feeling disconnected can leave us emotionally adrift, impacting not only how we view ourselves but also how we interact with the world. Belonging becomes an emotional anchor—a way to feel seen, valued, and supported as we navigate life's uncertainties.

Our environments play a crucial role in creating a sense of belonging. A warm and inviting home can reinforce bonds and create a sense of unity among its inhabitants. Similarly, workplaces, schools, and community spaces focused on inclusion and collaboration encourage people to feel engaged and connected.

Creating a Sense of Belonging in Home Design
A well-designed home is more than just a physical structure—it's a space where belonging is cultivated. When a house is intentionally designed to reflect its inhabitants' values, personalities, and needs, it becomes a sanctuary where everyone feels seen and supported.

Shared spaces like dining rooms and living rooms are prime opportunities to design for connection. Arranging furniture that encourages conversation, incorporating meaningful objects like family photos, and using warm, inviting colors can make these areas feel like the heart of the home. At the same time, personal retreats, like an art corner or a home office, acknowledge the need for individuality within a shared environment, allowing each person to feel valued.

The materials and elements we incorporate into our homes also play a role in creating belonging. Biophilic design, which brings nature indoors, brings a sense of connection to the world around us. Personal touches, like handmade decor or items with sentimental value, tell a story about the people who live there and make the space uniquely theirs.

By creating spaces that support relationships, honor individual identities, and promote a sense of togetherness, we turn our homes into environments where everyone feels valued and at peace. Belonging is not just a feeling; it is a foundation for thriving, and thoughtful home design makes it possible.

Belonging by Design: A Story of Transformation

When Shelly inherited her grandmother's old house, she wasn't sure she wanted it—it felt more like a relic of the past than a place she could call home. All the rooms were outdated, the furniture was mismatched and definitely not her style, and the walls were lined with dusty knickknacks and figurines. But something told her that she could make this house a space where she felt she truly belonged.

Determined to create a home that reflected her own identity and values while honoring her grandmother's memory, Shelly began a journey of transformation. She started small, asking herself how she wanted to feel in her home. Warm. Connected. Inspired. With that vision in mind, she rolled up her sleeves and got to work.

Creating Connection Through Design

One of her first projects was the living room. Shelly wanted it to feel like the heart of the home—a space where friends and family would naturally gather. She bought overstuffed furniture and arranged it to encourage conversation, placing the chairs and sofa in a semicircle around the fireplace. She added soft blankets and pillows in warm, earthy tones, bringing a sense of comfort and welcome to the space.

On the walls, Shelly replaced the old, faded artwork with a mix of family photos and her own paintings. Each piece told a story: a snapshot from a childhood beach trip, a watercolor she had painted during a difficult season of her life, a photo of her grandmother smiling in the garden. Every time she looked at the walls, she felt a sense of connection—to her past, her family, and her own journey.

Honoring Individuality in Shared Spaces
Shelly also wanted the house to reflect the unique personalities of the people who visited regularly. So she created a cozy reading corner for her sister, complete with a plush chair and a shelf of her favorite books. For her best friend, a musician, she designated a corner with a stool and a stand for her guitar, inviting impromptu jam sessions. These little touches made the home feel alive and inclusive, a place where everyone felt welcomed and seen.

Designing a Sanctuary for Belonging
One of the most transformative changes Shelly made was to the kitchen. For her grandmother, the kitchen had been the heart of the house, where love was shared through meals and conversations. Shelly wanted to honor that tradition while making it her own. She installed open shelving to display her grandmother's vintage tea sets alongside her own modern mugs. She painted the cabinets a soft green—a nod to her grandmother's favorite color—and added a farmhouse table that could seat all her loved ones.

The kitchen became a hub for connection. Hosting Sunday brunch turned into a weekly ritual. Laughter and the smell of fresh coffee and cinnamon rolls filled the air, and the space that Shelly was once hesitant about now overflowed with life.

The Transformation

As Shelly's work on the house continued, something beautiful happened: The house began to feel like her home. It wasn't just the new furniture, the fresh paint, or the curated decor—it was the way the space reflected her heart and her relationships. Every corner of the house carried meaning. The garden she planted in the backyard reminded her of summer afternoons with her grandmother. The gallery wall in the hallway told the story of the people she loved. The home did not just belong to Shelly—it was a space where everyone who entered felt they belonged too.

The Power of Belonging in Home Design

Shelly's journey is a testament to the power of intentional home design. A house is just a building, but a home is a space filled with connection, love, and belonging. By making thoughtful choices and having a meaningful vision, Shelly created a sanctuary where she—and everyone she welcomed—could thrive.

Belonging is about creating spaces that feel like an extension of who we are and what we value. It is about honoring the past while embracing the present. Most importantly, it is about opening our doors to connection, turning a house into a home where everyone feels they truly belong.

Relational Strategies: How We Communicate

Communication Strategies for a Home Remodel

A home remodel can be an exciting opportunity to create a space that reflects shared dreams, but it is also a potential minefield for miscommunication and conflict. Effective communication strategies are essential for ensuring that everyone feels heard, valued, and involved in the process. Here are key strategies:

1. **Set Clear Goals Together:** Discuss and agree on the purpose of the remodel. What do you want the space to achieve? Is it more about functionality, aesthetics, or both?
2. **Define Roles:** Avoid misunderstandings by clarifying who is responsible for specific decisions and tasks.
3. **Engage in Active Listening:** Take time to genuinely hear each other's ideas, concerns, and preferences. Validate differing perspectives.
4. **Be Willing to Compromise and Be Flexible:** Be willing to meet in the middle. It is unlikely both people will get exactly what they want in every instance, so prioritize shared goals.
5. **Schedule Regular Check-Ins:** Set aside time to review progress, adjust plans, and address concerns before they escalate into frustration.

Transformational Story: Remodeling a Marriage Along with the Home

When Sharon and Ben decided to remodel the kitchen in their 1960s ranch house, they thought it would be fun and bring them closer together. But as the weeks dragged on, disagreements began to pile up. Sharon envisioned a sleek, modern kitchen with minimalist cabinetry, while Ben dreamed of rustic charm with reclaimed wood and open shelving. What started as lighthearted debates escalated into tense standoffs. Neither felt heard, and the remodel began to symbolize the growing divide in their relationship.

One night, after a particularly heated argument about tile choices, Sharon suggested they sit down and redefine their approach. After doing a little research, and shedding a few tears, they developed a set of communication strategies that they used to guide the remainder of their remodel—and, unintentionally, to rebuild their connection.

- **They started with a shared vision.** They worked on a vision board together, and by blending their ideas, they found a cohe-

sive style that honored both their preferences: a modern farmhouse look. This collaborative effort gave them a clear direction and eased their earlier frustration.
- **They defined roles.** Ben took charge of sourcing materials for structural elements like wood and flooring, while Sharon focused on the aesthetics, like color palettes and decor. Clear boundaries reduced overlap and arguments.
- **They practiced active listening.** During weekly check-ins, they each shared their top priorities and concerns. Ben learned that Sharon's minimalist kitchen reflected her need for order and simplicity, while Sharon realized Ben's preference for rustic elements stemmed from his desire for a warm, welcoming home. Understanding these deeper motivations helped them find creative compromises.
- **They stayed flexible.** When a reclaimed wood vendor fell through, Ben pivoted and chose a different option that complemented Sharon's modern vision. Meanwhile, Sharon agreed to incorporate a reclaimed wood dining table as a focal point, blending their styles seamlessly.

By the time the remodel was complete, their kitchen reflected not just a harmonious design but also a newfound strength in their relationship. It became their favorite place, blending sleek cabinets with rustic accents that honored both their styles. More importantly, they had honed their communication skills and learned how to support each other's ideas while prioritizing their shared goals.

Sharon and Ben's story shows that a home remodel is not just about transforming spaces; it is an opportunity to transform relationships. With clear communication, mutual respect, and a commitment to collaboration, a remodel can be a journey that brings people closer together, both in design and in life.

Developmental Changes and Life Transitions: Moving in Together
Life transitions, like moving in with a partner for the first time, can be both exciting and challenging. Developmental theories by psychologists Erik Erikson and Salvador Minuchin provide valuable insights into how to navigate these shifts. Erikson's stages of psychosocial development highlight the importance of intimacy and identity in early adulthood, when forming close, meaningful relationships is key to thriving. Minuchin's family systems theory emphasizes the need for clear roles and boundaries when two people create a shared living environment. Together, these two frameworks help us understand the emotional and relational dynamics at play during cohabitation and offer tools for building a harmonious partnership.

When couples move in together, they often encounter differences in habits, expectations, and values. Successfully navigating this transition requires open communication, flexibility, and mutual respect. The theoretical focus is on balancing individuality while creating a shared identity, all while managing the inevitable growing pains that come with merging lives.

A Transformational Story of Growth: Emma and Alex Move In Together
Emma and Alan were thrilled to take the next step in their relationship by moving in together. They envisioned cozy dinners, snuggling on the couch for movie nights, and sharing morning coffee in their sunny kitchen. But within a few weeks, their excitement gave way to friction. Emma was used to maintaining a spotless living space, while Alan was more laid-back about clutter. Alan enjoyed frequently inviting friends over, while Emma valued her quiet evenings. What had seemed like small differences at first began to snowball into big disagreements.

One night, after an argument about dishes left in the sink, Emma and Alan sat down to reflect. They realized that moving in together was not just about sharing a space—it was about building a new chapter of their lives. To make the transition smoother, they explored strategies rooted in Erikson's and Minuchin's theories.

- **Identity and Intimacy (Erikson):** Emma and Alan recognized that their conflicts stemmed from the fear of losing individuality in their shared space. They agreed to carve out personal areas in their home—a plush chair in the bedroom where Emma could sit and journal and a small desk for Alan's hobbies. These spaces gave them the freedom to recharge individually while still feeling connected.
- **Roles and Boundaries (Minuchin):** Inspired by Minuchin's focus on clear boundaries, they created a "roommate agreement" of sorts. They divided household responsibilities, like cleaning, cooking, and grocery shopping, based on their strengths and schedules. This helped minimize misunderstandings and gave both a sense of contribution and control.
- **Shared Rituals for Connection:** To foster intimacy, they created weekly rituals like a "Sunday reset," where they cleaned and organized together while listening to music. They also started a tradition of Friday night date nights, alternating who planned the evening. These rituals became anchor points in their relationship that reinforced their bond.

Over time, Emma and Alan found their rhythm. Their home reflected both their personalities—Emma's love for order and Alan's flair for creativity merged into a warm, inviting space. More importantly, they developed stronger communication skills and a deeper understanding of each other's needs.

The Transition as Growth
Emma and Alan's story illustrates how moving in together can be not just a logistical challenge but a developmental milestone. Erikson

reminds us that intimacy thrives when individuality is respected, while Minuchin emphasizes the importance of clear roles and boundaries in shared systems. By approaching cohabitation with openness, patience, and intentionality, couples can turn the challenges of this life transition into opportunities for growth, resulting in a home and a relationship that feels uniquely theirs.

Developmental Design: A Teenager's Journey Toward Independence Through Room Design
Adolescence is a critical period of growth, when teenagers begin asserting their independence and forming their identity. Developmental theories, such as Erik Erikson's "identity versus role confusion" stage, emphasize the importance of this phase in helping teens discover who they are. Providing a safe space for self-expression, like allowing them to design their bedroom, can play a significant role in supporting this process. It's not just about aesthetics; it's about giving your teenager the autonomy to create a space that reflects their emerging personality while maintaining a sense of belonging in the family system.

Salvador Minuchin's family systems theory also highlights the importance of balance: teenagers need the freedom to explore their individuality, but they still need clear boundaries and a sense of connection within the family. Letting them design their room can become a powerful tool for achieving this balance.

A Story of Growth: Lily Finds Herself Through Room Design
Lily was 15 when she began to feel like her childhood room no longer fit her. The pink walls, cartoon posters, and fairy lights that once made her happy now felt childish and out of place. One day, after refusing to let her friends into her room out of embarrassment, Lily asked her parents if she could redesign her space.

Her parents were initially hesitant, but they recognized this was a moment for Lily to assert her independence. With guidance rooted in Erikson's and Minuchin's principles, they approached the project as an opportunity for growth—both for Lily and their relationship with her.

1. **Freedom Within Limits:**
   They gave Lily a budget and allowed her to create her own plan for the redesign. She spent hours researching color schemes, furniture ideas, and decor that felt more like "her." She chose deep green walls, minimalist furniture, and a gallery wall of her artwork. Allowing her to make these decisions helped her feel in control while still respecting family boundaries like the budget.

2. **Support and Collaboration:**
   Lily's parents helped her with the practicalities, like measuring the room, selecting durable furniture, and planning a timeline for the redesign. They worked together to repaint the walls and assemble furniture, turning the project into a shared experience that deepened their connection. This collaboration helped Lily feel supported without her parents taking over.

3. **Balancing Independence and Belonging:**
   While the room became a sanctuary of self-expression, Lily's parents made sure she still connected with the family. They created a rule that while her room was her space, she was still expected to participate in family dinners and shared activities. Lily loved being able to retreat to her new oasis when she needed alone time, but the family's support reminded her she was not isolated.

The Outcome

When the redesign was complete, Lily beamed with pride. Her room reflected her evolving identity—a space filled with bold colors, personal touches, and functional design for both studying and relaxing. More importantly, the process had strengthened her relationship with her parents. They had shown her that they respected her growing independence while remaining a source of support and guidance.

Lily's story illustrates how room design can be more than just a makeover—it can be a developmental milestone. Parents can turn a simple room redesign into a meaningful step toward independence, identity, and stronger family bonds by respecting their teenager's need for autonomy while providing structure and collaboration.

Family Systems: Generational Living—Bowen

When extended family members, such as in-laws, move into a shared home, it can create unique challenges and opportunities for growth. **Bowen family systems theory** provides valuable insights into navigating these dynamics. Bowen emphasized the importance of balancing emotional connection with individuality, or differentiation of self, in family relationships. Maintaining this balance is critical when multiple generations live under one roof, since overlapping needs, habits, and expectations can lead to conflicts. Designing an in-law suite—a dedicated living space for extended family members—can help establish healthy boundaries while maintaining emotional closeness (Bowen 2017).

Family Systems: The In-Law Suite

The real purpose of an in-law suite goes beyond practicality; it is about creating an environment where each generation feels respected and valued. It provides privacy and autonomy for the in-laws while ensuring they remain integral to the family system.

An in-law suite is more than just a convenience; it encourages harmony in multigenerational living. By providing space for independence while encouraging connection, families can navigate the complexities of generational living with grace and mutual respect. Bowen family systems theory reminds us that with clear communication, healthy boundaries, and intentional design, generational living can strengthen family bonds and create a supportive, enriching home for everyone.

A Transformational Story of Growth: The Coopers and Their New Multigenerational Home

When Joan and Ben Cooper learned that Ben's aging parents needed to move in due to health concerns, they had mixed emotions. While they were eager to help, they worried about the impact on their family dynamic. Their two young children thrived on routine, and Joan, who worked from home, valued her quiet space. Adding two more adults to the mix seemed daunting.

After evaluating their needs and available space, the Coopers opted to create an in-law suite in their home's unused basement. Guided by principles from Bowen family systems theory, they approached the transition with intentionality and a focus on maintaining harmony.

1. Balancing Connection and Independence
The Coopers designed the in-law suite for both autonomy and inclusion. The suite included a bedroom, bathroom, small kitchenette, and a cozy seating area. This setup allowed Ben's parents to maintain their routines, like preparing their own breakfast or enjoying quiet afternoons, without feeling entirely dependent on the rest of the family.

At the same time, shared spaces on the main floor, like the dining and living rooms, were redesigned to encourage connection. Over time, family meals became a cherished tradition, offering opportunities to connect while allowing Ben's parents to maintain their independence the rest of the day.

2. Clarifying Roles and Boundaries
To prevent misunderstandings, Joan and Ben had an open discussion with Ben's parents about household expectations. They agreed on responsibilities, such as the grandparents helping with light childcare duties and contributing to meal prep, while Joan and Ben managed the broader household responsibilities. This approach, inspired by Bowen's emphasis on clear roles, helped everyone feel valued and respected.

3. Managing Emotional Triangles
One of Bowen's key concepts is "emotional triangles," where tensions between two people are deflected onto a third. Recognizing this dynamic, the Coopers committed to directly addressing any issues. For example, if Ben's mother disagreed with Joan about the kids' routines, they discussed it openly rather than involving Ben as a go-between. This approach built trust and minimized unnecessary friction.

4. Honoring Individual Needs
Each family member had space to recharge and express their individuality. The grandparents decorated their suite with photos and keepsakes; Joan turned a spare bedroom into a home office; and the kids got to express themselves in their dedicated playroom. These spaces helped everyone maintain their sense of self within the shared home.

The Outcome
Over time, the Coopers found a rhythm that worked for everyone. Ben's parents enjoyed their independence in the suite while cherishing time with their grandchildren. Joan appreciated having extra help with the kids, and the family grew closer through shared meals and weekend activities.

The in-law suite was not just a physical addition—it became a symbol of respect, boundaries, and togetherness. By designing the space with Bowen's principles in mind, the Coopers created an environment where all generations could thrive.

Positive Psychology, Mindfulness, and Life/Work Balance in the Home

Transformational Story of Generational Living and Balance for the Ramirez Family
When Carlos and Elena Ramirez welcomed Carlos's mother, Rosa, into their home, they did not anticipate how much the arrangement would test their work-life balance. Both Carlos and Elena were working remotely post-pandemic, juggling demanding jobs while parenting their two children. Adding Rosa introduced new dynamics—some enriching, others challenging. With everyone now sharing the same space for living, working, and caregiving, tensions over privacy, interruptions, and time management quickly surfaced.

Drawing inspiration from mindfulness practices and positive psychology, the Ramirezes intentionally approached these challenges. By focusing on balance, clarity, and gratitude, they transformed their household into a harmonious, functional space that supported the well-being of every family member, even amid their crazy schedules.

Rachel Lynn Melvald

Creating Work-Life Harmony in a Multigenerational Home

1. Mindful Design for Workspaces

Carlos and Elena prioritized creating dedicated workspaces within their home so they could maintain productivity while minimizing stress. They converted a spare bedroom and part of the garage into separate home offices and added soundproofing, comfortable furniture, and personal touches to make the spaces inviting. They created a small seating area within Rosa's in-law suite where she could relax, ensuring she had her retreat as well.

By clearly delineating "work zones" and "family zones," the Ramirezes reduced interruptions and created a positive sense of structure. This mindful separation also allowed them to mentally transition between work and home life, a practice shown to reduce burnout and improve focus.

2. Family Rituals to Strengthen Bonds

To offset the pressures of their busy schedules, the family adopted simple, intentional rituals that nurtured connection. Drawing from positive psychology's emphasis on gratitude and well-being, they began each morning with "family gratitude time," where everyone shared one thing they were thankful for. This practice set a positive tone for the day and helped them stay connected, even during hectic moments.

In the evenings, Rosa led a mindful cooking routine with the children, teaching them traditional recipes while focusing on the pleasure of preparing meals together. These rituals became a cornerstone of the family's day and helped them balance work demands with quality time.

3. Time Boundaries and Communication

Work-life balance requires clear boundaries, especially in a multigenerational home. Carlos and Elena established quiet hours during their workdays so Rosa and the children knew when they were unavailable. Rosa took on a larger role during those hours, keeping the children engaged with educational activities or outdoor play.

To avoid resentment or misunderstandings, the family held regular family check-ins to review what was working and what needed adjusting. This open communication reinforced mutual respect and kept frustrations from escalating.

4. Mindful Breaks and Self-Care
Understanding the importance of mindfulness for mental health, Carlos and Elena incorporated short breaks into their workdays. Whether it was a quick walk in their backyard garden with Rosa or a five-minute breathing exercise, these mindful pauses helped them reset and return to their work with renewed focus.

Rosa, too, benefitted from these practices. She joined Elena for yoga sessions in the evenings and began a gratitude journal, a habit that gave her the opportunity to reflect on the joys of living with her family. These moments of self-care enriched the household atmosphere, leading everyone to feel calmer and more grounded.

The Transformation
As the weeks went by, the Ramirezes found a rhythm that worked for everyone. The designated workspaces allowed Carlos and Elena to stay productive, while the family rituals and mindful practices brought everyone closer. Once worried about being a burden, Rosa found a renewed sense of purpose in supporting her son's family and passing down traditions to her grandchildren.

Their home became a place where work, life, and relationships coexisted in harmony. The challenges of balancing multiple roles—remote work, caregiving, and family time—were no longer overwhelming but were opportunities for connection and growth.

The Lesson: Mindfulness and Positivity in Work-Life Balance

The Ramirezes' story demonstrates how mindfulness and positive psychology can transform the challenges of multigenerational living into opportunities for deeper connection and greater well-being. By creating boundaries, fostering gratitude, and prioritizing self-care, they achieved a work-life balance that enriched their relationships and daily lives.

In a world where the boundaries between work and home are increasingly blurred, intentional living reminds us that balance is not just about managing time—it is also about creating harmony within ourselves, our work, and the people we love.

Improving Productivity and Creativity in the Home Space

Our home environments profoundly impact how we think, feel, and work. A well-designed home space can fuel productivity, spark creativity, and support a sense of purpose, whether tackling a work project, enjoying a creative hobby, or managing daily tasks. Science shows that environmental factors like lighting, layout, and even color choices influence focus, energy, and innovation. We can transform our homes into hubs of inspiration and efficiency by intentionally designing our spaces to align with these neurodesign principles.

A Story of Transformation: Marc's Creative Awakening

Marc was a freelance graphic designer who loved his work, but he found it challenging to stay productive at home. His desk was in a corner of the living room, which meant he was constantly surrounded by noise, clutter, and distractions, and his creativity felt stifled. Recognizing the toll these disruptions were taking on his work and mental health, he decided he needed to make a change.

Marc started by clearing out an underused spare room and converting it into a dedicated office. He painted the walls a calming shade of blue to encourage focus and positioned his desk near a window to take advantage of natural light, which boosted his mood and energy level. To spark creativity, Marc incorporated biophilic elements, including a living wall of plants and a small water feature, creating a connection to nature that helped him feel grounded and inspired.

Once he had his new room situated, organization was his next priority. Marc invested in shelves and storage solutions to keep his supplies within reach but out of sight. Decluttering his workspace minimized mental distractions, helping him to focus more easily on his projects. He added a whiteboard so he could brainstorm ideas visually.

The results were transformative. Marc found he was more productive with a dedicated, intentional space. He completed projects faster and with more creativity, which rekindled his passion for design. The simple act of rethinking his home environment improved his work and ignited his enthusiasm for his craft.

The Takeaway
Marc's story illustrates how thoughtful design can unlock productivity and creativity at home. By addressing variables like lighting, organization, and inspiration, anyone can create a space that supports their goals and sparks their imagination. Whether it is a small desk in a corner or a dedicated home office, deliberate design can turn any space into a personal powerhouse for success.

Jung: Actualization and Transformation—Using Lineage, Symbols, and Art as Transformation
Carl Jung's work delves into the profound journey of self-actualization and transformation—a process of aligning the conscious and unconscious parts of the psyche. Jung believed that this journey was deeply tied to lineage, symbols, and the transformative power of art. By connecting with the archetypes embedded in our collective unconscious, we can tap into a wellspring of wisdom that elevates

our sense of purpose and creativity. Symbols, whether in dreams, mythology, or art, serve as gateways to understanding our inner world and unlocking our full potential. Similarly, embracing our lineage—our familial and cultural heritage—grounds us in our identity while propelling us toward growth.

Art, in Jung's view, is not just a creative expression but a sacred act of transformation. It externalizes our internal experiences and brings the unconscious to light, allowing us to integrate fragmented aspects of ourselves and find meaning in the complexities of life. By engaging with symbols, lineage, and art, we embark on a transformative path toward self-actualization, finding elevation in the process of becoming whole.

A Story of Transformation: Sophia's Journey to Wholeness

Sophia was a talented artist, but her creativity had been blocked for years. She felt disconnected from her art and unsure of her purpose. When her mother passed away, she inherited a box of family heirlooms: faded photographs, handwritten letters, and a peculiar collection of embroidered symbols that her grandmother had created. Although she did not understand their significance, Sophia felt drawn to these artifacts, sensing they held a hidden message waiting to be uncovered.

At a friend's suggestion, Sophia began studying Carl Jung's theories on symbols and the collective unconscious. She noticed that the embroidered patterns resembled archetypal symbols—images that carried universal meaning across different cultures and eras. These same symbols had appeared frequently in her dreams, which she had ignored for years. Sophia began journaling about the symbols and her dreams, feeling a growing connection to her family's lineage and the stories passed down through generations.

One evening, while handling the heirlooms, she had a breakthrough. The symbols on the embroidery were connected to her grandmother's life story—a tale of resilience, creativity, and self-reinvention during a time of great adversity. Inspired by this discovery, Sophia decided to weave these symbols into her art. She began painting again, creating vivid works that blended her grandmother's motifs with her own abstract style. As she painted, Sophia felt as though she were channeling not only her own emotions but also the strength and wisdom of her ancestors.

Through this process, Sophia experienced what Jung would describe as individuation—the integration of her conscious and unconscious selves. Her art became a way to honor her lineage while forging her own path. Over time, she reclaimed her creativity and found a deeper sense of purpose and identity. She held her first solo exhibition, calling it "Roots and Wings," a nod to the balance between grounding oneself in heritage and soaring toward self-actualization.

The Takeaway
Sophia's story demonstrates how engaging with heritage, symbols, and art can affect our lives. By exploring her unconscious through Jung's principles, she discovered her path to self-actualization and creative rebirth. Her journey shows us that personal transformation isn't always about becoming someone new—it is about uncovering and integrating the richness that's already inside us. Symbols, art, and our ancestors' stories can guide us on this path, elevating our lives and inspiring us to reach our fullest potential.

PART III
Neurodesign Elements for Harmonious Living

Designing a harmonious home based on environmental psychology involves creating an environment that nurtures individual well-being while encouraging healthy relationships among those who live together. Key design elements include maximizing natural light to enhance mood and social interaction, choosing calming colors to promote tranquility, and adding natural elements like plants to reduce stress and encourage connection. Open, flexible layouts facilitate movement and interaction, while comfortable textures invite relaxation and ease. Adding personal touches like meaningful decor strengthens emotional bonds, and managing sound and scent enhances the overall atmosphere. By integrating these elements, we can create spaces that are comfortable for everyone and promote peaceful coexistence and joyful living. The chapters in this part take an in-depth look at each design element and how it is applied in real homes. Through examples and case studies, we'll explore neurodesign elements that transform a space and promote healing for the inhabitant or the system.

The Origins of Environmental Psychology

Environmental psychology posits that our surroundings have an impact on how we think and feel. It's like when we walk into a room, we feel a good or bad vibe. This "vibe" is an exchange from outside stimulation, such as lighting and sound, registered in the body-brain system. This includes, in its most primitive forms, how we perceive threats and how we react in either fight, flight, or disassociation (Bell and Sundstrom 1966). In other words, our environment affects us deeply. According to Bell and Sundstrom, environmental psychology, with its focus on how the environment affects the functioning of individuals, groups, and organizations, has existed for over 30 years. These environmental factors include climate, pollution, architecture, lighting, sound, and smell, as well as parental or societal messages that influence how we think and feel.

Environmental psychology gained traction from a study of hospital design that looked at the therapeutic impact of layout, furniture design, and color (Sommer and Osmond 1960). The interior design and architecture purportedly had a positive therapeutic influence on the patient. Furthermore, environmental psychology was strengthened in its application to the design of residential, office, and institutional spaces, extending to the design of more significant communities. The foundation of the study of environmental psychology is reflected in Osmond's (1957) hypothesis that seating arrangements can affect social interaction. An example of how furniture design impacts socialization can be seen in Sommer and Ross's (1958) study, in which rearranging chairs to face one another versus in the center of the room was shown to promote human interaction.

Design Psychology and the Home Environment

The home embodies how we carry ourselves socially, emotionally, and developmentally in many aspects of our lives. Israel's 2003 study identifies the significant role of the home in how it is held in people's minds as a "home" versus a "residence." Home qualities were differentiated in terms such as "community, privacy, self-expression, personal identity, and warmth" (Israel 2003, 347). The study questioned the origins of the feelings of "home" and how they can be ascribed to space (Smith 1994). Israel (2003) purported that the concept of home eliciting feelings of safety goes back to childhood experiences of past spaces and can be conscious preferences, not emotional ones.

The home not only provides safety and shelter, but in today's world, since the pandemic, the home is also a hybrid living-work space responsible for fulfilling multiple functions and commanding more creative ways to draw boundaries in space and synthesize our daily activities around the rooms that hold specific functions. Gosling (2013) claimed that manipulating spaces can alter the activities performed in the rooms. For example, the placement of the couch and chairs in a living room can promote connection and intimacy, the arrangement of appliances and utensils in a kitchen can encourage cooking, and the position of beds in bedrooms can support sex and intimacy. Gosling further showed that other aspects of environmental psychological design variables, such as lighting, can also influence ambience-altering mood.

Other studies point toward home environments as a significant area of research across disciplines, citing studies from sociology, anthropology, geography, history, architecture, and philosophy (Mallett 2004). The concept of home has cross-cultural influences that include variables such as gender, family, house, haven, and traveling between home and work and other locations. Home is said to be rooted in psychological processes, as scholars have pointed out that spatial design can increase or detract from social connection and intimacy, power dynamics, and shifting roles that are defined by the function of the home environment. Functions of the home further support psychological processes such as the basic needs of safety, security, social connection, and relaxation. It is a touchpoint and acts as a safe harbor in the secure attachment where individuals can feel free and safe to explore, knowing they can return to restore. The home also sets the stage for cognitive and social development by encouraging family interactions that promote cognitive processes, language development, and socialization (Mallett 2004).

Israel (2003) details research on ambiance in an illustrative study on the existence of home and self-regulation. Home can be a place of safety and security, but it can also function as a threat and place of insecurity. The study notes a survey where participants were asked to identify the most critical emotions or perceptions they wanted to evoke in themselves and others when entering 18 different rooms or spaces. They selected two ambiances from 29 options that included qualities such as organization, privacy, rejuvenation, and tranquility. The most selected ambiances were "inviting" (chosen by 95% of participants for at least one space), "organization" (85%), and "relaxation" (70%). However, the distribution of these ambiances varied by room. For instance, the "inviting" ambiance was most frequently chosen for the entryway (54%), front porch (48.5%), and guest room (47%), but it was less commonly selected for other spaces (Israel 2003).

The findings, while showing unanswered questions, reveal two significant conclusions. The first one shows the psychological processes that operate in the home, and the second study demonstrates the wealth of research that would benefit from further studies on how ambiance plays a role in social interactions in the house, thus expanding the connection of home psychology to the broader fields of how to manipulate the environment. The environment can be manipulated through sound and texture. Different environments can induce psychological states, such as the beach experience touching on sand, water, and warm weather, which can affect relaxation in its preexisting environment. Other environments, like moving to a new neighborhood that is replete with a tree line and free from crime versus a neighborhood plagued with police activity and other variables such as crime and lack of safety measures, illustrate how the broader environment, such as the community at large, affects psychological processes. (Israel 2003).

Neurodesign was born from fundamental principles found in architectural history, such as biophilia, ergonomics, proxemics, color theory, temperature, materials, sound, and lighting. Understanding these central concepts can help us gain insight into how our spaces can shape us. Distilling these theories and the degrees to which we can apply them to our ways of living and the spaces surrounding us further enhances our well-being.

7

Biophilia, Ergonomics, Proxemics, and Spaces of Refuge

Biophilia: Nature as Flow

"Bio" means life, and "philia" means "friendly feeling toward," so "biophilia" can be defined as our natural tendency to want to commune with and be surrounded by nature. In its most basic sense, we are attracted to primitive forms in nature and space (Fromm 1973).

As Kara Rogers notes:

> Anecdotal and qualitative evidence suggests that humans are innately attracted to nature. For example, the appearance of the natural world, with its rich diversity of shapes, colors, and life, is universally appreciated. . ..
>
> Some of the most powerful evidence for an innate connection between humans and nature comes from studies of biphobia

(the fear of nature), in which measurable physiological responses are produced upon exposure to an object that is the source of fear, such as a snake or a spider.

Rogers explains that because fear enabled survival, humans had a fundamental connection with nature (K. Rogers, n.d.).

It can be argued that biophilia, in its most primitive form, lives in our subconscious or, in Jungian terms, in our collective unconscious as a defensive response pattern to offset threatening species. Yet, we can, in Freudian defensive terms, simulate this defensive response as an adaptive one to support our fight-or-flight tendencies in a positive direction by, for example, facing our desks toward the door so we can see if somebody is approaching. Or, looking at nature outside and viewing the movement of the wind and the trees can have a natural regulatory function. Placing your desk near a window to take advantage of nature provides a regulatory function by calming the nerves and aiding focus. Other treatments can include bringing in various natural shapes of household plants. It can be as simple as an orchid placement, with its silhouette producing a calming effect.

Biophilic design is rooted in the concept that people have an innate connection to nature, a theory supported by Wilson's (1984) biophilia hypothesis, which posits that humans have an inherent tendency to seek connections with nature and other forms of life. This connection has been extensively studied in environmental psychology and neuroscience, revealing that incorporating natural elements into built environments can lead to significant health benefits. Research has shown that exposure to nature, even within an indoor setting, can lower cortisol levels, reduce stress, and improve cognitive function (R. Kaplan and S. Kaplan 1989).

The presence of natural elements in the workplace or home can contribute to a state of physiological relaxation, as indicated by research from Ulrich et al. (1991), who found that patients recovering from surgery in hospital rooms with views of nature had faster recovery times and required less pain medication compared to those facing a blank wall. The concept of prospect and refuge, first introduced by Appleton (1975), aligns with the biophilic approach, suggesting that people prefer environments where they can both survey their surroundings and find protection. Positioning one's desk to face a door, for instance, aligns with this principle by creating a psychological sense of safety and preparedness, which can reduce stress and increase productivity.

Neuroscientific research supports the idea that biophilic design can regulate the autonomic nervous system. For example, studies on attention restoration theory (ART) propose that natural settings help the brain recover from cognitive fatigue by engaging involuntary attention, allowing for better focus and problem-solving abilities (Kaplan 1995). Additionally, exposure to fractal patterns found in nature, such as tree branches and waves, has been linked to reduced physiological stress responses and increased alpha brainwave activity, which promotes relaxation (Taylor et al. 2011). Beyond visual exposure, the multisensory aspect of biophilia plays a significant role in psychological well-being. Soundscapes that mimic nature, such as birdsong or flowing water, have been shown to lower blood pressure and enhance mood (Alvarsson et al. 2010). Similarly, touching natural materials like wood or stone can evoke a grounding effect, further contributing to emotional regulation (Kellert and Calabrese 2015).

In urban environments, where access to green spaces may be limited, integrating biophilic principles into architectural and interior design is essential for facilitating mental resilience. Green walls, indoor gardens, and increased daylight exposure through skylights or large windows are effective strategies for enhancing well-being in high-density settings (Kuo 2015). Moreover, the concept of "restorative environments" suggests that spaces designed with nature in mind can facilitate faster recovery from psychological stressors, benefiting both mental and physical health (Hartig et al. 2014).

Studies on workplace productivity further illustrate the benefits of biophilic design. Research conducted by Nieuwenhuis et al. (2014) found that office environments enriched with plants led to a 15% increase in worker productivity and a significant reduction in perceived stress. The physiological benefits of plants in indoor settings are due to improved air quality, higher humidity levels, and enhanced psychological comfort, creating a more supportive work environment (Dijkstra et al. 2008).

Residential settings that incorporate biophilic elements also demonstrate positive outcomes in emotional regulation and social cohesion. Access to private green spaces or well-designed communal courtyards has been linked to lower crime rates and higher social engagement in urban housing developments (Sullivan and Kuo 2007). These findings reinforce the belief that biophilia is not merely an aesthetic trend but a deeply ingrained biological need with far-reaching implications for health and community well-being. Biophilic environments have also been explored as therapeutic tools in the context of trauma recovery. Trauma-informed design integrates natural materials, soft lighting, and organic textures to create spaces that promote a sense of security and comfort. This application highlights the role of biophilia as a design philosophy as well as a fundamental component of emotional healing.

A Story of Renewal: Marla's Balcony Transformation

Marla lived in a downtown high-rise and worked long hours from home. Recently, she had been feeling increasingly drained by her urban lifestyle. Her apartment was functional, but it wasn't warm and inspirational. On a whim, she bought a variety of potted plants, hanging pots overflowing with colorful flowers, and a small fountain that mimicked the sound of a babbling brook, transforming her small, unused balcony into a biophilic sanctuary. The transformation was simple but profound. Marla now had a restful outdoor area where she could spend her breaks and mornings surrounded by greenery and sunlight. She noticed her stress levels decrease and her creativity soar during work. Her balcony became more than a retreat; it was a space of renewal, reminding her of nature's power to restore balance and flow.

Ergonomics
Ergonomics is "an applied science concerned with designing and arranging things people use so that the people and things interact most efficiently and safely" (*Merriam-Webster*, n.d.a). Ergonomics is especially important to highlight as a design principle because it supports how our bodies connect, adjust, and move within our interior space. Perhaps most associated with office space, the alignment of your office chair with respect to your eyeline with your computer screen promotes healthy posture, aids in productivity, and prevents health conditions such as carpal tunnel syndrome. As we arrange furniture, install cabinetry, and hang our art, we can be mindful of how we relate our senses to the objects we view, touch, and feel. For example, hanging pictures to align with our eyeline allows us to view the piece without straining to look up or down. Another interior design ergonomics trick can be seen in installing kitchen cabinetry on the horizontal line.

Beyond visual alignment, ergonomic principles extend to optimizing movement and comfort within the home through furniture placement and selection. The placement should encourage ease of motion, ensuring that occupants do not need to overextend or strain their bodies. Research has shown that improper furniture arrangements can contribute to musculoskeletal disorders, particularly in individuals who spend prolonged periods in static postures (Dul and Weerdmeester 2008). A well-designed space considers body mechanics, such as ensuring that seating areas provide lumbar support and that frequently used furniture is positioned to minimize repetitive strain (Parcells et al. 2010).

Seating is a crucial aspect of ergonomic design. Chairs should support the natural curvature of the spine, promoting a neutral posture that reduces stress on the lower back. Adjustable chairs with lumbar support, padded armrests, and breathable materials enhance comfort and prevent physical strain (Gaggioli 2020). Sofas and lounge chairs should also be carefully chosen, ensuring that the seat height allows feet to rest flat on the floor to prevent unnecessary pressure on the knees and lower back (Vischer 2008).

In dining areas, table and chair heights should be proportional to ensure comfortable seating postures. A standard dining chair should allow your feet to rest flat on the floor while having your elbows at a 90-degree angle when using the table. Misalignment in these dimensions can lead to discomfort and long-term strain on the shoulders and wrists (Pheasant and Haslegrave 2006).

Bed ergonomics is another essential consideration in home furniture design. Mattresses should provide sufficient support to maintain spinal alignment and be made with materials that distribute body weight evenly to prevent pressure points. The height and firmness of a bed frame should also allow ease of movement, especially for individuals with mobility issues.

Storage furniture should also be designed with ergonomics in mind. Drawers and shelves should be placed within a comfortable reaching distance to minimize bending and straining. Cabinets positioned too high or too low force individuals to adopt awkward postures that can lead to chronic discomfort (Dul and Weerdmeester 2008). Incorporating pull-out shelves and soft-close drawers can further enhance ease of use and accessibility.

A Story of Alignment: Jack's Work-From-Home Upgrade
Jack, a software engineer, spent long hours at his desk and often ended his day with back pain and fatigue. After consulting with an ergonomic expert, he made adjustments to his workspace—he replaced his dining chair with an adjustable office chair, repositioned his monitor to eye level, and incorporated a standing desk converter. The results were immediate: his pain subsided, his focus improved, and he felt more energized throughout the day. Jack realized that investing in how he situated himself was not just about comfort—it was about setting himself up for success.

Proxemics
The next psychological design principle to employ is the notion of proxemics. Proxemics is defined as "the study of the nature, degree, and effect of the spatial separation individuals naturally maintain (as in various social and interpersonal situations) and of how this separation relates to environmental and cultural factors" (*Merriam-Webster*, n.d.b).

As the definition states, the importance of our boundaries and space can determine many degrees of our healthy relational functioning. As we use the term "boundaries" in psychological terms, we can acknowledge how crucial they are to positive self-esteem and relationships. Maintaining boundaries in our budgets and bodies, and to the degree that others can support or violate us, becomes crucial to our well-being. Much is so in our own space and spaces in our homes. Applying proxemics can nurture harmonious relationships by the degree to which individuals, couples, and families are comfortable and thriving in their spaces. Examples can be found in a she shed or a man cave where one can escape, dwell, and create independently. However, too much separation can lead to isolation or loneliness, which is why it is essential to commune with family and friends, hence, the purpose of a living room.

Proxemics speaks to the form and function of each room in our homes. Each room can elevate and enliven our creative pursuits while supporting connection and harmonious living. Proxemics, as a psychological design term and the function of a boundary and space, encourages well-being, harmonious relationships, and elevated lifestyles.

The psychological effects of room design have been studied extensively, with research showing that well-planned spatial arrangements can influence behavior, productivity, and stress levels (Altman 1975). The ability to control spatial boundaries has been linked to increased self-efficacy and personal agency (Gifford 2014). For instance, designated spaces for relaxation, such as reading nooks or meditation areas, contribute to emotional regulation and cognitive restoration. In contrast, multifunctional spaces that allow for social interaction and collaboration, such as family rooms or shared workspaces, support collective engagement and creativity (Steele 1980).

The cultural dimension of proxemics also plays a role in how space is perceived and utilized. Different societies have distinct norms regarding personal space, with some cultures favoring close physical proximity and others emphasizing greater spatial separation (Hall 1966). Understanding these cultural variations can inform the design of spaces that respect diverse needs, particularly in multicultural households. Research suggests that when individuals feel their spatial preferences are respected, their overall satisfaction and psychological well-being improve (Stokols 1972).

Incorporating proxemics into home design allows for an adaptable living environment that aligns with the psychological needs of its inhabitants. Whether creating separate retreats for solitude or open, inviting communal areas, thoughtful spatial planning can enhance both individual well-being and collective harmony. By acknowledging and implementing proxemics principles, homeowners and designers can create spaces that support not only aesthetic appeal but also the fundamental human need for balanced interaction and privacy. For instance, in families where individuals have clearly defined personal spaces, such as separate workstations or reading areas, there is less reported conflict and a higher sense of autonomy. This suggests that physical boundaries in shared environments contribute to relationship satisfaction and personal well-being (Kellert 2015).

Proxemics plays a significant role in child development, as the spatial arrangement and organization of a child's home environment influence their ability to develop independence and self-regulation skills. Research suggests that well-structured, spatially considerate home designs provide children with the necessary stability and predictability to foster self-discipline and autonomy. Clark and Uzzell (2002) emphasize the impact of environmental affordances on adolescent behavior, noting that the home, neighborhood, and school settings shape developmental outcomes. When children are provided with dedicated areas for learning, playing, and sleeping, they develop stronger cognitive and social skills. Research in education and environmental psychology suggests that the way space is arranged can either support or hinder a child's ability to focus and engage in developmental tasks (Maxwell 2006). Therefore, proxemics should be considered when designing children's bedrooms, study areas, and communal play spaces. For example, neighborhoods with accessible communal spaces, such as parks and shared courtyards, encourage social interaction while still respecting individual property lines and privacy needs. These findings reinforce the idea that personal space and communal connectivity should be balanced not just within homes but also in broader community planning efforts (Gehl 2010).

As technology continues to shape how we use and experience space, digital proxemics has emerged as an area of interest. The rise of remote work and virtual meetings has led to new considerations in home design, where dedicated workspaces must coexist with living areas without disrupting household harmony (Carayon et al. 2020). Research suggests that creating clearly defined work areas, separate from leisure or sleeping spaces, enhances productivity and reduces work-related stress (Koenig 2018). This highlights the evolving role of proxemics in adapting to modern lifestyle needs.

A Story of Balance: Ella and Mia's Shared Apartment
Ella and Mia, best friends and now roommates, clashed over the shared spaces in their apartment. The living room felt like neutral ground, but the kitchen and dining area became sources of tension. After learning about proxemics, they rearranged their apartment to define more explicit boundaries: Ella set up a small coffee station in her bedroom, while Mia claimed a reading corner in the living room. They also redefined shared areas by scheduling designated quiet hours and mealtimes. This rebalancing between shared and personal space transformed their relationship, bringing more independence and intimacy.

8

Our Spaces and Our Senses

We experience the world through our senses, and the spaces we inhabit can either stimulate or soothe them. By understanding how sensory elements like color, light, sound, and texture influence us, we can create homes that look beautiful and feel supportive and balanced. This chapter explores how intentional design can activate or calm our senses, transforming our spaces into environments that align with our emotional and physical needs.

Musicology
Most of us feel connected to music because it can penetrate the subconscious, allowing us to access and play out our emotional lives. Music can heal, uplift, transcend, and create what is deemed "ambiance" in the neuroscience community—creating a mood or effect in an environment or an "atmosphere." While "ambiance" and "atmosphere" are often used interchangeably, they have subtle differences,

particularly in design. Ambiance refers to the specific mood, tone, or emotional feeling created within a space through sensory elements like lighting, sound, color, and decor. It is about the immediate sensory experience and emotional reaction you feel when entering a room—such as a cozy, intimate, or energizing environment. Atmosphere, on the other hand, is a broader term that encompasses a space's overall environmental quality or character, including its physical setting, temperature, air quality, and more. While ambiance contributes to the atmosphere, the atmosphere is the more significant, more encompassing feeling of a place, shaped by both its sensory elements and physical characteristics. Essentially, the ambiance is a key component that helps shape the atmosphere, but the atmosphere includes the overall feel of the space.

When we visit a spa and attune to the relaxing music, we can unwind, float, and de-stress. De-stressing occurs when the nervous system combines the sympathetic nervous system (activation) and parasympathetic nervous system (deactivation and relaxation) so the body is open to connection, relaxed, and hungry. Music can elicit any emotion, and there are many theories as to whether there is an authentic primordial sound, such as found in "OM," or how memory, learning, and cognition play a role in relationship to the rhythm of the music connecting us to our memories.

Fundamentally, significant research supports the beneficial effect of music on cognition, memory, and emotional regulation. Research has shown that music profoundly impacts the brain, influencing cognitive, emotional, and memory functions. Listening to music engages multiple brain regions, including the hippocampus and amygdala, which are critical for memory and emotional responses, and stimulates the brain's reward system, releasing dopamine and evoking pleasure. Studies suggest music can improve cognitive functions, enhance motor skills, and even promote neurogenesis—the formation of new neurons. It has also been linked to emotional regulation, helping individuals manage stress, alleviate symptoms of depression, and induce positive feelings.

Furthermore, music has therapeutic applications, such as in dementia care, where familiar songs improve mood, communication, and overall quality of life. The emotional power of music also influences memory, with research indicating that music can modify how we recall past events, often infusing them with emotional elements. Collectively, these findings highlight music's potential to enhance mental health, foster well-being, and positively transform the brain (Harvard Medical School 2023).

The neuroscience of sound explores how our brain processes sound and its profound effects on our emotions, cognitive functions, and overall well-being. When sound enters the ear, it is converted into electrical signals processed by the brain, allowing us to identify things like pitch, volume, and tone. Sound activates areas of the brain that influence emotional responses, such as the limbic system, which is why music and certain sounds can make us feel happy, relaxed, or even sad. Calming sounds, like nature noises or soft music, have been shown to reduce stress and promote relaxation by triggering the parasympathetic nervous system, helping lower heart rate, and easing tension (Kallinen and Ravaja 2007). Additionally, sound can improve focus and productivity by using specific music or binaural beats to enhance concentration, creating an environment that fosters mental clarity and creativity. The brain is also flexible, meaning it can adapt to new sounds or music, which is why therapeutic sound-based interventions, such as those used for people with Parkinson's disease, can help improve motor skills and emotional regulation.

In home design, this understanding of the neuroscience of sound can be leveraged to create environments that support mental and emotional health. For example, integrating calming sounds, such as water features, ambient music, or nature sounds, can increase relaxation and reduce stress in living areas or bedrooms. In home offices or workspaces, soft background music or binaural beats can improve focus and productivity by encouraging a state of relaxed alertness. Sound-conscious design can also enhance communication and interaction within the home with well-placed acoustic treatments—like rugs, curtains, or soft furniture—that reduce noise and improve speech clarity. Sound can also help strengthen the emotional connection to space by incorporating familiar or comforting sounds that evoke positive memories and feelings. For those with specific needs, like cognitive impairments or neurological conditions, sound can be incorporated therapeutically to aid in motor coordination, memory, or emotional well-being. Ultimately, sound plays a crucial role in home design by influencing a space's atmosphere, functionality, and emotional resonance, thereby improving its inhabitants' overall quality of life.

Sensory Relaxation and Stimulation: Nikki, Joseph, and Lucas's Story

Nikki and Joseph were eager to create a home environment that supported their autistic son, Lucas. He would often have a meltdown when he became overwhelmed by bright lights, chaotic sounds, and overly stimulating textures. After attending the Intentional Design Summit, Nikki and Joseph learned how to design a sensory-friendly space that balanced stimulation and relaxation.

They installed warm, adjustable LED lighting in Lucas's playroom, which provided a calming atmosphere. They added soft rugs and beanbags with comfortable textures that soothed his nervous system and hung noise-canceling panels on the walls to reduce disruptive sounds. Nikki and Joseph also added a sensory corner with tactile toys and a bubble lamp for visual stimulation when Lucas needed focus. These intentional changes met Lucas's unique sensory needs and created a harmonious environment for the whole family.

Color Psychology: Creating Mood States in the Home

Color Theory
Now ubiquitous in the understanding of how color affects mood, color theory can be applied in various neuroscientific ways in our households to create safe, productive, and creative spaces that inspire mindful and cooperative living. Since its inception, color theory has been understood through the lens of Isaac Newton, who, in 1666, determined how light fractures into a prism of colors (Fraser and Banks 2004), how the retina processes and codes the perception of color, and how light and pigment affect the penetration of color. We can look at theories of color as systems held by theorists, such as in the classic color wheel, complementary colors found in the Munsell Color Tree (Fraser and Banks 2004), and color schemes used by artists dating back to the Bauhaus.

Color psychology stipulates that color influences moods, physiology, and behavior. Colors can be applied to promote safety and create more optimal environments for productivity and creativity. Colors can promote healing and relaxation as well as activate and enliven. Colors also have cultural meaning. Empirical research on color theory is scant, but a 2020 study by Jonauskaite et al. titled "Universal Patterns in Color-Emotion Associations Are Further Shaped by Linguistic and Geographic Proximity" evaluated a large number of color associations and found universal qualities of colors have universal emotional associations, as shown below:

- Black: 51% of respondents associated black with sadness
- White: 43% of people associated white with relief
- Red: 68% associated red with love
- Blue: 35% linked blue to feelings of relief
- Green: 39% linked green to contentment

- Yellow: 52% felt that yellow signified joy
- Purple: 25% reported they associated purple with pleasure
- Brown: 36% linked brown to disgust
- Orange: 44% associated orange with joy
- Pink: 50% linked pink with love

Choosing which colors are right for you and your space and how to integrate them for optimal functioning requires an individualized approach related to color psychology. It is not a one-size-fits-all approach. While a color may have a universal value, how people interpret and relate to color is very individual. So just because purple is your favorite nail polish color, that doesn't mean you want your living room walls painted purple. Color is an art and science that can seem overwhelming, but working with a design professional can make it less daunting and exciting.

A Story of Vibrancy: Amanda's Kitchen Revival
Amanda, a chef and food blogger, wanted her kitchen to feel energizing and creative, and she realized the drab beige walls weren't doing her any favors. After consulting a color expert from True Color, she painted the walls boldly yellow, a color known to evoke energy and positivity. She complemented it with green accents that symbolized freshness and vitality. The transformation was immediate—Amanda felt more inspired while cooking, and her kitchen became a hub of creativity and warmth for her family and guests.

Lighting: Shaping Mood and Energy

Lighting
Lighting significantly affects how we feel in a space. Bright, cool light can invigorate us, while warm, dim light can cause relaxation. Just as color theory claims to have a psychological impact, so can lighting. Lighting as a design variable can perform aesthetic

functions of shaping, spotlighting, contrasting, and creating shadow effects, and as a pure survival function of allowing us to see in the dark to offset threats. Lighting plays a significant role in mood and affect regulation, sleep cycles (such as circadian rhythms), and overall well-being and health. As light can modulate brightness and hue, it can also alter our mood states. Lighting can have a calming and relaxing effect, thereby reducing stress. It has been shown to reduce depression scores as well as increase cognitive functioning. It can alter our moods and support productivity and creativity. It can highlight textures and patterns that mimic or elicit memory states.

Lighting has three components: brightness, hue, and saturation. Adding color to lighting affects mood states, while the directionality can further impact psychological, cognitive, and behavioral functioning. Binarities, such as feeling small or large, exposed or private, relaxed or tense, and concentrated or expansive, can be evoked by lighting. A designer can employ and modulate lighting sources to elicit these psychological effects. A study by Tomassoni et al. (2016), titled "Psychology of Light: How Light Influences the Health and Psyche," provided guidelines for improved health and wellness when exposed to light in a specific environment. They argue that light is a "cognitive map" and a driver of perception, eliciting human responses confounded by memory states. Living artfully is being intentional in how light directs attention and mood and enlivens our spaces. For example, a design philosophy and model such as the Danish concept of hygge exemplifies the use of lighting to enhance well-being. Hygge employs warm, soft lighting as well as soft textures to induce contentment through coziness and comfort.

A Story of Comfort: David's Evening Escape

A graphic designer, David often struggled to wind down after long workdays. His living room, lit by harsh overhead LEDs, felt more like an office than a relaxing place. After consulting a lighting expert, David installed layered lighting: floor lamps with warm bulbs for ambient light and dimmable sconces for reading. This new setup transformed his evenings, making it easier for him to transition from work mode to relaxation.

Sound: Creating Harmony in the Home
Sound shapes our experience of space, from calming background noise to energizing rhythms. It can either soothe our nerves or create subtle stress. Research in environmental psychology suggests that auditory experiences significantly impact mood, cognitive performance, and physiological well-being (Jahncke et al. 2011). By thoughtfully designing our home environments to manage sound, we can create a space that enhances relaxation, productivity, and overall harmony.

The Science of Sound and Well-Being
The way sound interacts with our surroundings can influence our emotional and physical state. Exposure to excessive noise has been linked to increased stress levels, disrupted sleep, and decreased concentration (Basner et al. 2014). Conversely, carefully curated soundscapes, such as soft instrumental music or nature sounds, have been shown to promote relaxation and improve cognitive function (Alvarsson et al. 2010).

Neuroscientific research supports the idea that sound affects brain function. Studies indicate that exposure to calming sounds, such as waves or birdsong, can lower cortisol levels and activate the parasympathetic nervous system, which is responsible for relaxation and recovery (Loewy 2020). On the other hand, constant exposure to environmental noise, such as traffic or loud household appliances, can lead to chronic stress and an increased risk of cardiovascular disease (Munzel et al. 2018).

The Role of Acoustics in Home Design

A well-balanced acoustic environment enhances comfort and mental well-being. Interior designers and architects use principles of sound absorption, reflection, and diffusion to create spaces that support their intended auditory experiences (Blesser and Salter 2009). Incorporating biophilic design elements into indoor environments has been shown to positively influence human physiology and cognitive functions. For instance, a study by Joye (2007) discusses how biophilic architecture can enhance psychological well-being by reducing stress and improving cognitive performance. Soundproofing techniques, such as insulated walls and double-pane windows, can further enhance privacy and reduce external noise pollution, which has been linked to improved sleep quality and reduced stress (Babisch 2014).

Sound as a Tool for Relaxation

Intentional soundscapes can transform a home into a tranquil sanctuary. Research in music therapy has demonstrated that slow-tempo music with minimal percussion induces relaxation and lowers blood pressure (Labbé et al. 2007). White noise machines, commonly used in nurseries and bedrooms, mask disruptive environmental sounds and promote restful sleep (Stanczyk 2011).

Incorporating nature sounds into the home environment has been shown to boost mental health. A study by Alvarsson et al. (2010) found that participants who listened to nature sounds after a stressful task recovered more quickly than those who listened to urban noise. Fountains, indoor water features, or digital soundscapes mimicking rain or ocean waves can help recreate these effects within a home environment (Grizka et al. 2020).

Enhancing Focus and Productivity Through Sound

For those who work from home, sound can be a crucial factor affecting concentration and efficiency. Research suggests that moderate ambient noise levels can enhance creativity and problem-solving skills by promoting a relaxed yet alert mental state (Mehta et al. 2012).

The Emotional Impact of Personalized Soundscapes

Sound is deeply tied to personal memories and emotional well-being. Studies suggest that familiar music has the ability to evoke nostalgia, improve mood, and reduce anxiety (Saarikallio 2011). Peretz and Zatorre (2005) provide an extensive review of the neural architecture dedicated to processing music. They discuss how distinct brain regions are specialized for various aspects of music perception, including melody, rhythm, and harmony. The study highlights the involvement of both cortical and subcortical structures in music processing and emphasizes the brain's capacity to adapt to musical training. For families, shared musical experiences can strengthen bonds and create meaningful traditions. Singing together, playing instruments, or curating a family playlist promotes connection and shared joy (Hargreaves and North 2008).

The Future of Sound in Home Design

Emerging technologies are revolutionizing how we integrate sound in our living spaces. Smart home systems now allow for customizable sound environments, adjusting background noise levels based on time of day, mood, or activity. Sound-based wellness interventions, like binaural beats and guided meditations, are gaining popularity for their potential to enhance mental clarity and relaxation (Lane et al. 1998). As neurodesign research advances, the integration of sound into home environments will continue to evolve. The recognition of sound as a fundamental design element underscores its role in creating harmony, well-being, and overall life satisfaction.

A Story of Harmony: Lila's Calming Playlist

Lila, a yoga instructor, noticed her home felt chaotic during busy mornings with her three children. After consulting with a musicologist, she curated playlists designed to elicit different moods. She played gentle, melodic tunes during breakfast to set a calm tone for the day and upbeat rhythms in the afternoon to energize the family. Each bedroom got a white noise machine, which helped everyone get restful sleep. By integrating sound intentionally, Lila brought harmony to her bustling household.

Texture: The Power of Touch in Home Design

The textures we surround ourselves with—soft fabrics, smooth surfaces, or rough materials—have a direct impact on how we feel. They can comfort, ground, or stimulate us, making texture an essential consideration in intentional design. Research in environmental psychology shows that sensory experiences, including touch, play a crucial role in emotional regulation and well-being (Ackerman et al. 2010). By consciously choosing textures to incorporate into our living spaces, we can create environments that support relaxation, focus, and even social connection.

How Texture Influences Emotion and Well-Being

Different textures elicit different psychological responses. Soft, plush fabrics like velvet or cashmere evoke warmth and security, making them ideal for bedrooms or reading nooks (Harlow and Suomi 1970). Rough textures, such as exposed brick or natural wood, can provide a sense of grounding and stability, reinforcing a connection to nature (Kellert and Calabrese 2015). Smooth surfaces, like polished stone or glass, can feel sleek and modern but may also come across as cold or uninviting when overused.

Studies have found that texture influences not just comfort but also social behavior. For instance, research by Ackerman et al.

(2010) revealed that people who sat on hard chairs were more rigid in negotiations, while those sitting on soft seating were more open to compromise. This suggests that textures can subtly affect how we interact with others, reinforcing the importance of mindful material selection in shared areas such as dining rooms and living rooms.

Creating a Balanced Sensory Experience

To achieve a harmonious home, it's important to mix textures thoughtfully. A balance of soft and firm materials can prevent a space from feeling overly sterile or excessively cluttered. For example, a living room with a plush rug, linen curtains, and a leather couch provides a diverse sensory experience that feels inviting yet structured. Interior designers often use layering techniques—combining various materials such as knitted throws, woven baskets, and sleek surfaces—to create visual and tactile richness that enhances comfort (Gifford 2014).

The role of nature-inspired textures in home design is particularly noteworthy. Biophilic design principles emphasize the integration of natural elements, including materials that mimic those found in nature, such as rough-hewn stone, raw wood, and plant fibers (Kellert and Calabrese 2015). These materials have been shown to lower stress and increase feelings of calmness, similar to spending time outdoors (Ulrich et al. 1991). Bringing these textures into the home can replicate the soothing effects of nature, promoting relaxation and contentment.

Texture and the Sense of Touch in Daily Life

Our sense of touch is often overlooked in interior design, but it plays a key role in shaping our daily experiences. The sensation of walking barefoot on a plush rug versus cold tile first thing in the morning can set the tone for the day. Soft bedding with high-thread-count sheets has been shown to improve sleep quality by reducing sensory disturbances (Cajochen et al. 2011). Even making small changes, such as adding a textured throw blanket or incorporating soft lighting that complements the tactile environment, can make a meaningful difference in how we experience our homes.

In spaces where focus and productivity are paramount, textures should be chosen with intention. Research suggests that excessive smoothness or synthetic materials can create a sense of detachment, whereas organic textures can promote mental engagement and creativity (Mehta and Zhu 2009). This is why many modern workspaces incorporate wooden desks or textured wall panels to counteract the sterility of tech-heavy environments.

A Story of Comfort: Maya's Cozy Retreat
Maya, a journalist working from home, realized her workspace felt cold and uninviting, which wasn't conducive to doing her best writing. Inspired by a design expert, she introduced textured elements: a plush area rug, a soft throw blanket, and a velvet chair. These changes made her office feel welcoming and safe, improving her focus and reducing stress during long writing sessions.

The Takeaway
Our senses are integral to how we experience and interact with our homes. By designing spaces that thoughtfully engage sight, sound, touch, and other sensory elements, we can create environments that support our well-being, enhance productivity, and foster deeper connection. Whether through calming textures, vibrant colors, or harmonious sounds, intentional design has the power to transform our spaces—and our lives.

Orientation, Organization, and Personalization

Orientation: Positioning Ourselves for Well-Being

How we orient ourselves in our space—where we place furniture, how we position ourselves in relation to light, and even how we face natural elements—can profoundly impact our mood and how well we function. Research in environmental psychology highlights that spatial orientation affects cognitive performance, emotional well-being, and overall comfort in our homes (Gifford 2014). By thoughtfully arranging our surroundings, we can enhance our ability to focus, relax, and interact.

How we position ourselves in a room influences our sense of security and ease. Studies show that people prefer seating that has a clear view of the entrance, a principle known as prospect-refuge theory (Appleton 1975). This is why many people instinctively position their desks facing a doorway or choose seating arrangements that allow them to see the whole room. Having a sense of control over our environment reduces stress and helps us feel more grounded (Kaya and Weber 2003).

Orientation also plays a role in how we interact with others. In dining and living areas, circular or semicircular seating arrangements encourage conversation and social bonding (Sommer 1969). In contrast, linear seating, such as side-by-side arrangements, is more suited to independent activities or focused tasks. Understanding these principles can help us design spaces that support either solitude or connection, depending on our needs. Positioning workspaces near windows enhances focus and energy levels, while situating relaxation areas to avoid direct glare creates a more soothing environment (Veitch and Galasiu 2012).

The placement of artificial lighting also affects mood and behavior. Warmer lighting promotes relaxation and is best suited for bedrooms and living rooms, whereas cooler lighting enhances alertness and productivity, making it ideal for workspaces (Boyce 2014). Adjustable lighting solutions, such as dimmer switches or layered lighting with a mix of task, ambient, and accent lights, allow for greater flexibility in adapting a space to fit different needs.

How furniture is arranged dictates movement patterns, usability, and comfort within a home. Research suggests that cluttered or poorly arranged spaces can increase cognitive load and stress, making it harder to focus and relax (Vohs et al. 2013). Open layouts with clear pathways reduce friction in daily activities, making movement more intuitive and comfortable.

Incorporating ergonomics into spatial orientation also enhances well-being. Seating with proper lumbar support and workspaces with appropriate desk heights prevent physical strain, while positioning frequently used items within easy reach minimizes unnecessary exertion (Dul and Weerdmeester 2008). These small but significant adjustments contribute to long-term comfort and efficiency in the home.

Biophilic design emphasizes the importance of incorporating nature into living spaces. Research has shown that views of greenery can lower stress, boost creativity, and improve overall well-being (Kellert and Calabrese 2015). Positioning seating areas to face outdoor landscapes or placing mirrors strategically to reflect natural light enhances these benefits, making spaces feel more open and connected to the outside world (R. Kaplan and S. Kaplan 1989).

Indoor plants, natural materials, and water features can also introduce elements of nature into the home. Even small adjustments, such as setting up a reading nook near a sunlit window or placing a desk where it offers a view of trees, can significantly impact relaxation and focus (Ulrich et al. 1991). These simple design choices harness the power of nature to support mental and physical health.

Ultimately, how we arrange and orient ourselves in our homes shapes how we experience daily life. Thoughtful placement of furniture, intentional use of light, and incorporation of natural elements all contribute to a home that feels supportive and rejuvenating. By paying attention to spatial organization, we can design environments that promote well-being, productivity, and meaningful social interactions.

A Story of Energy: Liam's Sunlit Workspace

Liam was a writer who found himself feeling lethargic and uninspired in his home office. After consulting an expert on natural energy flow, he repositioned his desk to face a window where morning sunlight streamed in. He added reflective surfaces to amplify the light and incorporated shades to control glare during peak hours. These small adjustments made a big difference in his energy level, which was just the boost Liam needed to write with renewed focus and enthusiasm.

Wayfinding: Moving Through Space Effortlessly
Wayfinding is the art and science of how we navigate through our environments. Thoughtful design makes movement intuitive and stress-free, which is especially important for those with cognitive challenges. Research in environmental psychology has shown that clear and consistent spatial cues help reduce anxiety and increase confidence in navigating a space (Passini et al. 2000). For individuals with dementia or neurodivergent conditions, wayfinding strategies such as color-coded paths, distinct landmarks, and unobstructed sightlines improve orientation and independence (Marquardt and Schmieg 2009).

The wayfinding process relies on a combination of visual, auditory, and tactile cues to create a seamless experience. Effective signage, contrasting colors, and good lighting are essential elements that guide movement and prevent confusion (Arthur and Passini 1992). In home environments, clear pathways and intuitive room layouts ensure that residents can move comfortably without encountering unnecessary obstacles. Making simple modifications, such as ensuring that doorways are easily distinguishable or using textured flooring to indicate transitions between spaces, can significantly improve navigation and accessibility.

Incorporating natural elements into wayfinding design can also enhance spatial awareness. Studies suggest that exposure to natural light and organic forms supports cognitive function and reduces stress (Kellert and Calabrese 2015). Windows that provide a view of outdoor landscapes, for instance, can serve as orientation anchors and reinforce a sense of place (R. Kaplan and S. Kaplan 1989).

For public spaces, effective wayfinding is crucial in creating inclusive and accessible environments. Airports, hospitals, and senior-living facilities implement wayfinding principles to accommodate a diverse range of users, ensuring that individuals with varying cognitive and physical abilities can navigate these spaces with ease (Weisman 1981). Universal design strategies, such as clear sightlines, multilingual signage, and audible navigation cues, create equitable access and boost independence.

At home, personalized wayfinding strategies can enhance daily routines and provide a sense of security. Making simple adjustments such as placing frequently used objects in predictable locations or using motion-sensor lighting in hallways reduces cognitive load and makes navigation effortless (Mitchell and Burton 2006). By integrating wayfinding principles into interior design, individuals can experience greater autonomy and comfort in their living spaces.

A Story of Guidance: Dr. Morrison's Dementia-Friendly Home
When Dr. Morrison updated her mother's home to accommodate her cognitive decline, her main focus was on creating clear, navigable pathways. She used contrasting colors to highlight important areas, placed symbolic cues near rooms (like a photo of her mother near the bedroom door), and ensured there was ample natural light. These simple adjustments reduced confusion and gave her mother a greater sense of independence, transforming the house into a supportive, empowering environment.

Organization: Decluttering for Emotional Health
A clutter-free space is more than just about aesthetics; it also contributes to emotional clarity and healthier relationships. Decluttering can reduce stress, improve focus, and build connection. Research in environmental psychology indicates that excessive clutter can lead to cognitive overload, increased stress levels, and decreased productivity (McMains and Kastner 2011). Clutter creates visual and mental distractions, making it difficult for people to process information efficiently and maintain a sense of control over their environment (Vohs et al. 2013).

Decluttering has been linked to improved mental well-being and emotional resilience. Studies suggest that organized spaces promote a sense of calm and stability, which can lower cortisol levels and reduce anxiety (Saxbe and Repetti 2010). In relationships where individuals have different tolerances for disorder, shared clutter can contribute to tension and disagreements. Establishing household routines for organization and storage solutions can help create an environment where all inhabitants feel more at ease and engaged with one another (Neave et al. 2017).

The impact of clutter also extends to social interactions. A cluttered home can make individuals feel embarrassed or hesitant to host guests, leading to social withdrawal and reduced opportunities for connection (Ferrari and Roster 2018). On the other hand, a well-maintained space opens the door to hospitality, encourages shared experiences, and strengthens relationships. Decluttering, therefore, is not just about removing excess items; it is about creating a home that supports meaningful social interactions and emotional well-being.

Decluttering requires mindful decision-making about what to keep and what to discard. Research in behavioral psychology suggests that people often develop emotional attachments to objects, making it challenging to part with unnecessary belongings (Frost and Gross 1993). Using structured decluttering methods, such as the KonMari Method or the four-box approach, can help individuals navigate these emotional barriers and create a more intentional living space (Kondo 2014). Applying similar decluttering principles in home offices can create an atmosphere conducive to concentration and productivity, further emphasizing the importance of a well-organized working space.

By prioritizing organization and intentional design, individuals can cultivate environments that enhance well-being, strengthen relationships, and support overall life satisfaction. Decluttering is not just about removing physical items; it is a practice of creating mental space, gaining emotional clarity, and building a home that truly serves its inhabitants.

A Story of Simplification: Tara's Decluttered Living Room
Tara, an organizational consultant, often advised clients to simplify their spaces, but her own living room had become overrun with toys, papers, and knickknacks. After committing to taking her own advice and decluttering, she removed unused items and created dedicated storage solutions for her family's belongings. The process not only cleared the room, but it also improved her family dynamics, and the home became a welcoming space for connection and relaxation.

Memory and Personalization: The Stories Our Spaces Tell
Our homes hold the stories of who we are. The objects we keep reflect our ancestry, emotional history, and sense of identity; they anchor us to our narrative. Personal possessions are tangible representations of memories that create a bridge between past experiences and present living spaces. Research in environmental psychology suggests that people form attachments to objects that evoke nostalgia, reinforce self-identity, and provide a sense of continuity (Csikszentmihalyi and Rochberg-Halton 1981).

Studies show that surrounding ourselves with meaningful items enhances emotional well-being and fosters a sense of belonging (Dittmar 2011). Heirlooms, souvenirs, and personal artifacts remind us of significant moments in our lives and reinforce social connections by preserving shared histories (Kamptner 1995). Whether it's grandmother's quilt, a piece of art from a meaningful trip, or a childhood book collection, these objects offer comfort and stability.

Our homes also reflect how we see ourselves and how we want to be perceived. The way we curate our spaces—choosing minimalist decor, vibrant artwork, or rustic furniture—communicates aspects of our personality and values (Gosling et al. 2002). A home filled with books may signal intellectual curiosity, while a space adorned with plants and nature-inspired materials may indicate a deep appreciation for the environment.

Beyond individual identity, home design plays a role in intergenerational memory and storytelling. Research suggests that the act of passing down objects through generations strengthens familial bonds and provides a sense of cultural continuity (Fivush et al. 2011). Personalization in home environments can also serve as an anchor during times of transition, offering familiarity and stability in new or uncertain situations (Rubinstein and Parmelee 1992).

However, while memory and nostalgia can offer comfort, they can also have negative effects. Holding on to objects from the past sometimes reinforces emotional distress, making it difficult to move forward. Excessive sentimental attachment to physical possessions can contribute to clutter and hoarding behaviors, leading to increased stress and anxiety (Frost and Gross 1993). Nostalgia can also idealize the past in a way that creates dissatisfaction with the present, stirring feelings of longing and regret rather than comfort and continuity (Batcho 2007). For individuals who feel trapped by past memories, their home environment may become an emotional burden rather than a source of support (Sedikides et al. 2008).

The objects we choose to keep are not just decorations; they are symbols of our journey. By intentionally designing spaces that incorporate meaningful elements while being mindful of what serves us in the present, we create environments that nurture emotional security, strengthen identity, and enhance overall well-being. A balanced approach to nostalgia allows for reflection and connection while supporting growth and change.

Rachel Lynn Melvald

A Story of Heritage: Ancestral Roots in Nina's Home
Nina was a Native American artist who filled her home with objects that honored her lineage: pottery passed down through several generations, beadwork created by her grandmother, and paintings inspired by her tribe's stories. These items decorated her space and connected her to her heritage and identity. With guidance from the research of Dr. Sam Gosling, she learned how these personal artifacts reinforced her sense of self and helped create a home that celebrated her history while inspiring her future.

The Takeaway
Our homes are more than physical structures—they are dynamic environments that shape our emotions, creativity, and relationships. By understanding orientation, wayfinding, organization, and personalization, we can create spaces that reflect who we are and support our lifestyles. Each small, intentional change can transform our homes into sanctuaries of well-being and self-expression.

How Designers Can Support Wellness
The following are some examples of psychological considerations that designers can use to support clients' wellness.

Social affiliation. This is a person's sense of belonging and connection with others, which fosters community and support. A design application might be to create communal spaces, such as a cozy living room or open-plan kitchen, that encourage social interaction. These spaces can include comfortable seating arrangements that promote face-to-face communication, making family members and guests feel connected. A large dining table or a communal seating area in a backyard, where people can gather for meals or conversations, nurtures a sense of belonging and community.

Experiences of intimacy. People need the ability to share meaningful moments and emotional closeness with others, which enhances relationships. A design approach might be to incorporate intimate or private areas designed for personal or couple time, such as a small reading corner, a loveseat by a window, or a peaceful garden alcove. These secluded spaces offer opportunities for emotional closeness and shared moments, providing a physical setting where relationships can deepen and grow. Soft lighting, comfortable textures, and personalized décor further enhance the sense of emotional intimacy.

Believing that one has a choice. This involves the perception of autonomy and control over one's environment and decisions, promoting empowerment. One way to apply this would be to design flexible spaces that can be adapted for different purposes, such as multipurpose rooms or modular furniture that can be rearranged easily. For example, a home office can transform into a guest room or a play area that can be repurposed for meditation or exercise. This flexibility gives occupants the perception of control over their environment and the autonomy to make choices that suit their needs at any moment.

Emotional expression. People need opportunities to express their feelings and emotions, which contributes to mental health and feelings of authenticity. Designers might consider providing areas for creative outlets where individuals can express themselves, such as a dedicated art studio, a music room, or a journal-writing corner. Displaying personal artwork, family photos, or mementos in visible places can also allow for emotional expression. These design elements encourage authenticity and emotional health by allowing residents to express their inner thoughts and feelings through art, music, or other creative forms.

Sensory regulation. People need the ability to manage sensory inputs in their environment to maintain comfort and reduce stress. A design application might be to incorporate elements that help regulate sensory inputs, such as soundproofing, soft lighting or dimmable lights, and natural textures. Consider using thick curtains or rugs to minimize noise and natural materials like wood or stone to add tactile comfort. Adding plants or water features can help reduce stress and bring a sense of calm to the environment. These design choices help manage the sensory environment, making it easier for individuals to feel comfortable in their homes.

Positive beliefs about the self. Cultivating self-esteem and confidence leads to healthier interactions and relationships. Designers might include areas that promote self-care and personal reflection, such as a calming spa-like bathroom with soothing colors and soft textures or a meditation corner filled with crystals and essential oils. Spaces dedicated to hobbies or achievements—a craft room, workout area, or gallery wall of personal accomplishments—can boost self-esteem by serving as a daily reminder of one's abilities and talents.

Optimism about the future. A hopeful outlook on life encourages resilience and a positive attitude. A design application might be to create a vision board or inspiration wall in a home office or creative space where family members can post goals and display affirmations or plans. It could include areas for growth, such as a home library or learning space, which can symbolize the potential for progress and encourage a positive outlook. Bringing in elements of nature, such as greenery and natural light, can evoke a sense of renewal and growth.

Meaning of life. A sense of purpose and direction contributes to overall well-being and fulfillment. A way to apply this in design would be to create spaces that reflect personal values, purpose, and spirituality. This could include a meditation or prayer room, a family heritage wall displaying ancestral stories, or a dedicated space for philanthropic projects or volunteer work. Personal symbols of meaning, such as inspirational quotes, religious artifacts, or items related to family traditions, can serve as daily reminders and enhance a sense of fulfillment and direction.

Applying these design principles can transform a home into an environment that nurtures physical comfort and emotional well-being, relationship building, and personal growth. The goal is to create intentional spaces that contribute to balance, support human connections, and help individuals thrive in all aspects of life.

My work has the transformative power to collectively heal while supporting a harmonious design process that can continue to reflect people's higher selves. Healing is a lifelong and beautiful journey, and our environments must evolve alongside this process. Nothing is more fulfilling than seeing the transformation of healing pathology and actualizing potential in someone's life and seeing it reflected in their space. As a psychotherapist, I see healing as ultimately living one's most authentic life, where trauma is transformed into beauty, and that is ART!

10

Flexibility and Beauty

Our homes are living, breathing spaces that evolve with us. They adapt as our needs change, reflecting the fluidity of our lives and relationships. At the same time, homes are where we look for inspiration and beauty to feed our souls. Through flexible spaces, meaningful design, and personal expressions of art, we can create homes that transform and uplift us daily.

Flexible and Adaptive Spaces
Our homes must be adaptable to the stages of our lives, from welcoming a new child to supporting aging family members. Flexibility in design ensures that our living spaces can grow along with us. Research in environmental psychology suggests that homes designed with adaptability in mind reduce stress and enhance overall well-being by allowing for seamless transitions through life's various phases (Gifford 2014). For instance, multifunctional rooms that

can shift from being an office to a nursery or modular furniture that accommodates different needs provide practical solutions for evolving households (Brand 1994).

Open floor plans, adjustable lighting, and movable partitions are common strategies that promote flexibility in design. A well-designed home offers spaces that cater to different activities and emotional needs, whether it's a quiet retreat for reflection or a common area for social connection (Marcus 2006). Research has also shown that adaptable environments can help older adults stay independent longer, reducing the need for institutionalized care (A. Sixsmith and J. Sixsmith 2008). Designing homes with accessibility and adaptability in mind ensures that they remain functional and comfortable throughout life's transitions.

A Home That Evolves with Us
When we design our homes with flexibility and beauty in mind, we create spaces that support our evolving needs while enriching our experiences. Whether through adaptable layouts, awe-inspiring aesthetics, or artistic expression, our homes should be places that empower us to live fully and harmoniously. By embracing the principles of fluidity and beauty, we ensure that our living spaces continue to reflect and enhance the people we are becoming.

A Story of Growth: Denise and Daniel's Expanding Family
Denise and Daniel were excited to welcome their second child, but they were concerned about fitting their growing family into their two-bedroom apartment. With the help of a design expert, they addressed their space issues. They bought modular furniture, including a crib that converted into a toddler bed, and rearranged their open-concept living area to include a play area. Over time, they continued to adapt their home—Daniel's office space evolved into a study area for their older child, and foldable dining furniture made creating space for

family gatherings a breeze. Their home became a testament to how thoughtful, flexible design can meet changing needs without sacrificing comfort or style.

Inspiring Spaces of Awe

Beyond function, beauty plays an essential role in our psychological well-being. Studies show that experiencing aesthetically pleasing environments can trigger positive emotions, reduce stress, and increase creativity (R. Kaplan and S. Kaplan 1989). Spaces that inspire awe—whether through architecture, natural elements, or artistic expression—activate the brain's reward system and contribute to a sense of fulfillment (Keltner and Haidt 2003). This is why homeowners often feel a deep emotional connection to spaces that integrate beauty in a way that aligns with their personal values.

Bringing nature into our living spaces is one of the most effective ways to create a sense of wonder. The principles of biophilic design emphasize the importance of natural elements, such as sunlight, greenery, and water, in fostering emotional and psychological well-being (Kellert and Calabrese 2015). Large windows that frame scenic views, indoor gardens, and materials inspired by nature help create an environment that feels uplifting and restorative.

We deserve to live in homes that evoke a sense of abundance and wonder created by the objects, furniture, and design elements that resonate with us.

A Story of Transformation: Michael's Gallery of Awe

Michael, a retired teacher, wanted his home to feel like a sanctuary of inspiration. He worked with an interior designer to curate pieces that brought him joy: a large, sculptural bookshelf filled with his favorite novels, a stunning chandelier that cast playful shadows, and a gallery wall of vibrant artwork from his travels. Adding these elements made his home feel abundant and full of life. Every time he entered his living room, Michael felt a renewed sense of creativity and gratitude, reminding him that beauty has the power to transform daily living into something extraordinary.

Art and Beauty

Art and design serve as profound expressions of identity and transformation. Surrounding ourselves with art that resonates with us has been linked to increased happiness and cognitive stimulation (Smith 2014). Whether it's an intricate painting, a handcrafted sculpture, or a collection of meaningful objects, art personalizes our space and reflects our inner world. Research in neuroaesthetics suggests that engaging with art can help regulate our emotions and provide a sense of purpose (Chatterjee 2013). When we intentionally curate our environment with beauty, we build a deeper connection to ourselves and our surroundings.

Artistic design choices also influence how we experience a space. Thoughtful color schemes, textures, and spatial arrangements impact mood and perception, shaping how we interact with our home (Elliot and Maier 2014). The concept of "designing for joy" emphasizes that our spaces should serve our practical needs and also bring us pleasure and inspiration (Lidwell et al. 2010). By incorporating art and beauty into our homes, we create environments that enhance our daily lives.

Art and Beauty as Transformation

Art is deeply personal, and its presence in our homes creates connections, inspires reflection, and fosters transformation. Whether it is a painting, a handmade quilt, or a cherished sculpture, art brings beauty and meaning to our spaces. Research in neuroaesthetics suggests that exposure to art activates the brain's reward system, evoking emotions and enhancing cognitive engagement (Chatterjee 2013). Art has the power to elevate mood, stimulate creativity, and even reduce stress by offering a sense of personal expression and identity (Smith 2014).

The way we incorporate art into our living spaces reflects our values, experiences, and aspirations. Some people gravitate toward vibrant, energetic artwork that brings a sense of dynamism and excitement, while others prefer muted, contemplative pieces that create a sanctuary for introspection. Art allows us to tell our stories visually, providing glimpses into our history, culture, and emotional landscapes (Leder et al. 2014).

Beyond aesthetics, art influences spatial perception and interaction. Studies have shown that the strategic placement of artwork can impact movement patterns within a room, guiding attention and offering a sense of balance and harmony (Cela-Conde et al. 2011). Integrating images of nature, such as landscapes or botanical prints, can enhance well-being by invoking its restorative powers, which aligns with biophilic design principles (R. Kaplan and S. Kaplan 1989).

Art also plays a role in strengthening relationships within a home. Collaborative family artworks or collections gathered over time serve as conversation starters and sources of shared meaning. Research suggests that communal artistic experiences strengthen bonds and contribute to an enriched sense of belonging (Silvia and Brown 2007).

Ultimately, art transforms a house into a home, making spaces feel more authentic and alive. By intentionally filling our surroundings with pieces that resonate with us, we create environments that bolster inspiration, emotional depth, and a sense of fulfillment.

A Story of Expression: Priya's Healing Through Art

After experiencing a challenging year, Priya decided to use her home as a canvas for healing. She incorporated pieces of art that resonated with her journey—an abstract painting symbolizing resilience, a handcrafted ceramic vase representing fragility and strength, and her own photography that captured moments of joy. These objects turned her space into a reflection of her transformation and provided daily beauty and connection. Priya realized that art can tell her story and ground her in the present, no matter how it is defined.

Conclusion

Flexibility and beauty are not luxuries—they are necessities for creating homes that support and inspire us. Adaptive spaces grow with us, while awe-inspiring design and personal expressions of art provide daily moments of joy and connection. Together, these elements transform our homes into sanctuaries that reflect who we are and aspire to be. By embracing both practicality and beauty, we craft environments where life can flourish in all its stages and forms.

While this book primarily explores the psychology of design in our homes, these concepts resonate far beyond our personal spaces. The same principles of environmental psychology that affect our living spaces can and should extend to the broader community context. Our public spaces, workplaces, schools, healthcare facilities, and neighborhoods all stand to benefit from thoughtful, intentional designs that support well-being and connection.

When we honor the role of inclusive design, accommodating the needs of neurodiverse populations, the aging, and those affected by trauma, we shift from creating spaces that simply function to spaces that heal and empower. This has profound implications for urban development, community planning, and even policymaking, as we aim to create environments that nurture the health of all individuals, regardless of their backgrounds or challenges. These principles apply to everyone, ensuring that no one is left behind in the pursuit of healthier, more connected communities.

As you embark on your design journey, remember that these principles are not just tools for personal growth but can be the foundation for transforming communities. So design for health and connection—at home and in the world around you. For more insights and tools to support your design journey, visit www.psychitecture.com.

Acknowledgments

Just after finishing my first draft of this book, I learned that a significant supporter of my work and practice in design and psychology had passed away suddenly. My uncle Ezra Florey was an intellectual, professor, and thinker who, on every birthday and seasonal holiday, sent me a book on psychology and design that inspired and educated me on my path. He believed in my business of Psychitecture from its formation, and it is only fitting that this book be an homage to Uncle Ez. Sadly, I will not receive any more books from him, but *Neurodesign: The Art and Science of Harmonious Living* will continue to give, and hopefully, shine its light on spaces for years to come.

Appendix A
Neurodesign Principles Through the Lens of Maslow's Hierarchy of Needs

Creating a harmonious home goes beyond aesthetics; it involves designing a space that nurtures physical and psychological well-being. A home that aligns with Maslow's hierarchy of needs addresses the multifaceted layers of human needs, helping people thrive at every stage of their personal development. By incorporating neurodesign principles, which blend neuroscience, psychology, and design, this toolkit empowers you to design an environment that positively influences the mind and body. It goes beyond providing shelter—it creates a sanctuary that nurtures the whole self, promoting growth, fulfillment, and lasting well-being.

Rachel Lynn Melvald

Physiological Needs (The Foundation: Shelter, Food, Sleep)

Neurodesign Principle: Comfort and Ergonomics
Creating a harmonious home begins with meeting your basic physiological needs, including sleep, nourishment, and shelter. These elements directly impact your health, highlighting the importance of designing spaces that support these basic functions. Neurodesign focuses on comfort and ergonomics to ensure these needs are met and enhanced.

Ergonomic Furniture: Invest in ergonomic chairs, desks, and mattresses to promote physical health. For example, adjustable desk chairs can support optimal posture during work hours, and memory foam mattresses can improve sleep quality by aligning the spine and reducing pressure points. The kitchen, as the central hub for nourishment, should be designed for ease of use, incorporating intuitive layouts and efficient storage so that meal preparation is straightforward and streamlined, ensuring that it's a pleasurable and effortless experience.

Biophilic Design: Integrating natural elements is essential for both physical and emotional health. Neurodesign principles suggest that natural light boosts serotonin levels, which help regulate circadian rhythms and ultimately improve sleep. Additionally, indoor plants provide air purification and reduce stress, contributing to a sense of serenity and overall well-being. Incorporate water features, such as small fountains or aquariums, to promote tranquility by introducing soothing sounds that support relaxation.

Intelligent Climate Control: Temperature regulation is essential for achieving optimum sleep and comfort. Research shows that a cooler room temperature enhances sleep quality by synchronizing with your body's natural sleep cycle. Smart thermostats can help maintain optimal temperature levels throughout the day, ensuring comfort in every season. Additionally, incorporating high-quality air filtration systems can reduce allergens and pollutants, contributing to your overall well-being.

Safety Needs (Physical and Emotional Safety and Stability)

Neurodesign Principle: Security and Stability Through Structure
A sense of security is essential for maintaining both physical and emotional stability. Your home should be a safe haven that minimizes stressors and maximizes feelings of safety. Neurodesign focuses on creating predictability and structure in the living environment.

Clear Layouts and Defined Spaces: A cluttered or disorganized environment can certainly raise your anxiety level. But neat, well-organized spaces can reduce your stress and promote emotional security. The best way to maintain a sense of structure is to create distinct zones for work, leisure, and rest. This design layout will encourage focus and help reduce the cognitive load of constantly navigating chaotic spaces. Add a well-labeled storage system to reinforce order and create greater control over your environment.

Physical Security: In addition to emotional security, physical safety is critical. Installing safety features like smoke detectors and alarm systems and maintaining well-lit areas in high-traffic zones like hallways and stairs are some simple and practical precautions. These practical elements mitigate feelings of vulnerability and reinforce a sense of physical security. Additional elements such as smart locks and security cameras can further heighten a sense of protection while preserving easy accessibility for trusted occupants.

Calming Color Schemes: Research from neurodesign shows that specific colors can influence emotional responses. Soft, calming tones such as pastel blues, muted greens, and earth tones promote relaxation and tranquility. These colors can reduce anxiety and produce a feeling of safety and warmth. Textures also contribute to creating a soothing environment; by including soft fabrics and tactile surfaces, you can further reinforce feelings of comfort and stability.

Love and Belonging Needs (Relationships, Connection)

Neurodesign Principle: Social Spaces and Personalization
Humans have a deep need for connection, whether with family, friends, or even pets. A harmonious home fosters relationships and provides spaces that support social interaction and individual reflection. Neurodesign advocates for creating environments that support both community and personal expression.

Community-Centric Design: Your home's layout should include spaces for interaction—such as open-concept kitchens, dining areas, and living rooms—that encourage family and social engagement. Flexibility is a key feature of neurodesign; focus on furniture that can be rearranged to allow for group activities as well as quiet, individual time. Elements like a cozy fireplace, a communal dining table, or a designated game area can reinforce togetherness and shared experiences.

Personal Reflection Areas: Creating quiet corners for personal reflection, such as a reading nook or meditation space, allows for moments of solitude and self-awareness. These spaces support individual emotional needs and promote mental clarity. Calming music or aromatherapy in these spaces can further enhance relaxation and introspection.

Personalization Through Art and Décor: Neurodesign emphasizes the role of personalized décor in establishing an emotional connection with a space. Personal artwork, family photos, and meaningful objects create a sense of belonging. These elements are deeply tied to personal identity and strengthen emotional bonds with your home. Additionally, dynamic design elements like interchangeable artwork or modular shelving can keep spaces fresh as you grow and your interests evolve.

Esteem Needs (Self-Worth, Recognition, Achievement)

Neurodesign Principle: Empowering Design and Reflection
Esteem needs are fulfilled when we feel valued, respected, and recognized for our accomplishments. A home that promotes achievement and self-expression can boost your confidence and encourage growth. Neurodesign principles focus on empowering design elements that support self-worth and recognition.

Empowering Layouts: Design spaces that promote your productivity and creativity. A well-organized, aesthetically pleasing workspace supports inspiration and achievement. Surrounding yourself with nature-inspired décor and natural elements can enhance creativity and performance, making workspaces more inviting and motivating. Ergonomic seating, adjustable lighting, and ample desk space can transform your workspace into a zone of inspiration and focus.

Promoting Reflection and Self-Assessment: Mirrors, vision boards, or journaling stations can all serve as tools for self-assessment and personal growth. These spaces encourage you to evaluate your progress, set goals, and visualize your achievements. Incorporating motivational quotes or affirmations can reinforce positive self-perception and resilience.

Mindful Lighting: Lighting is a powerful tool for boosting productivity and mood. Adjustable lighting, such as task lighting for focused work and soft lighting for relaxation, supports creative and cognitive functions. Lighting can enhance your concentration and provide a calming effect after a productive day. Incorporating innovative lighting systems that adjust to circadian rhythms can promote overall well-being and sustained energy levels.

Self-Actualization Needs (Personal Fulfillment, Creativity, Purpose)

Neurodesign Principle: Dynamic and Purposeful Design
Self-actualization refers to the fulfillment of personal potential, creative expression, and the pursuit of purpose. Neurodesign supports this need by designing environments that inspire growth, creativity, and meaningful work.

Dynamic Creative Spaces: A home should provide spaces that encourage exploration and creativity. Designate areas for artistic expression, whether that's an art studio, music room, or writing desk. Flexible furniture that adapts to different uses allows you to explore and engage in different activities. An environment that accommodates hobbies and learning can lead to new passions and greater personal fulfillment.

Connection to Nature: Biophilic design is essential for mental clarity and self-actualization. Integrating nature-inspired elements like plants, natural wood finishes, and access to outdoor spaces can improve your cognitive function and promote a deeper connection to the environment, leading to a sense of well-being.

Conclusion: Nurturing Your Full Potential Through Design
By focusing on Maslow's hierarchy of needs, this toolkit helps you build a home environment that nourishes the full spectrum of human needs, from physiological comfort to personal fulfillment. Each section, grounded in neurodesign, shows how to create a living space that aligns with your body and mind, encouraging a lifestyle that promotes health, productivity, creativity, and emotional well-being. When implemented thoughtfully, these principles can lead to a home that supports your daily needs and encourages you to reach your highest potential.

Expanding on these principles, it is important to recognize that a harmonious home can be a powerful tool for emotional resilience and overall mental health. As we learn more about the role of the environment on mental health, it becomes clear that the spaces we occupy reflect and shape our inner worlds. For example, integrating personalized elements within the home fosters emotional bonds and reinforces identity, promoting a sense of autonomy and control that is crucial for mental well-being.

Creating a dynamic living space that grows with you can help foster a mindset of continuous self-improvement and exploration. Incorporating flexible design elements that adapt as needs change—such as adjustable lighting, multifunctional furniture, or evolving décor—ensures that the space remains a supportive environment throughout all phases of your life. This dynamic flexibility encourages not only a response to immediate needs but also a space that nurtures long-term development.

Moreover, the relationship between you and your home environment can be seen as reciprocal. While your home supports personal growth and fulfillment, you also play an active role in shaping the home. This continuous interplay between you and your environment further strengthens the sense of ownership, promoting confidence and reinforcing the space's need for self-expression and individuality. Neurodesign shows how the built environment reflects personal values, aspirations, and emotional needs, fostering a sense of harmony and wholeness.

Creating a home that nurtures these needs is not merely an aesthetic choice but an investment in your mental and physical well-being. With intentional design, each element of your space can empower you, encourage growth, and create a foundation for a fulfilling life. A harmonious home is not just a space to live in; it is a sanctuary that nurtures your mind, body, and spirit. By addressing the full spectrum of Maslow's hierarchy of needs through neurodesign, your home becomes a place of balance, growth, and emotional resilience. The environment actively supports your journey toward self-actualization with each design choice, from ergonomic furniture to personalized décor and natural elements. As you create a space that adapts to your evolving needs, you create an atmosphere that encourages self-reflection, creativity, and personal growth. Ultimately, your home can be a constant source of inspiration and well-being.

Appendix B
Harmonious Home Checklist and Toolkit

This checklist is designed to help you evaluate and enhance your living space using the principles in this book. Each section focuses on specific aspects of your home that can help promote psychological well-being and a sense of fulfillment. Use this checklist as a practical guide to help you align your home with the principles of neurodesign and create a space that supports your authentic self and enhances your quality of life.

1. Assessment of Current Space

- **Reflect on needs:** Identify the psychological needs your current space fulfills (e.g., safety, comfort, inspiration).
- **Identify barriers:** List any psychological barriers your space presents (e.g., clutter, poor lighting, uncomfortable layout).

2. Intentional Design Elements

- **Natural light:** Ensure spaces have ample natural light; consider window treatments that enhance brightness.

- **Color palette:** Choose colors that evoke desired emotions (e.g., calming blues, energizing yellows).
- **Furniture arrangement:** Arrange furniture to promote conversation and flow; ensure it reflects how you want to use the space.
- **Personal touches:** Include artwork, photographs, or items that resonate with your identity and values.

3. Creating Zones of Purpose

- **Designate areas:** Identify areas for different activities (e.g., relaxation, work, creativity) and design them accordingly.
- **Mindful decor:** Use decor that inspires or brings joy; avoid items that feel heavy or burdensome.

4. Connection to Nature

- **Plants and greenery:** Incorporate indoor plants or flowers to enhance air quality and bring life to your space.
- **Natural materials:** Use materials like wood, stone, and fabrics that create a sense of connection to the outdoors.

5. Comfort and Well-Being

- **Comfortable furniture:** Invest in ergonomic furniture that supports physical well-being.
- **Cozy textiles:** Add soft textiles like throws, pillows, and rugs to create warmth and comfort.

6. Mindful Space Maintenance

- **Declutter regularly:** Schedule time to declutter and organize your space to promote a sense of calm.

- **Create a cleaning routine:** Establish a routine for keeping your space clean and inviting.

7. *Personal Reflection Spaces*

- **Mindfulness area:** Designate a space for meditation, reflection, or journaling that is quiet and peaceful.
- **Creative outlets:** Ensure there's a space for creative activities (e.g., art supplies, musical instruments) that reflect your interests.

8. *Community and Relationships*

- **Social spaces:** Create inviting areas that encourage gathering and connection with family and friends.
- **Shared spaces:** If living with others, discuss how to design shared spaces that respect everyone's needs.

9. *Future Planning*

- **Vision board:** Create a vision board that reflects your ideal living space and the feelings you want to evoke.
- **Long-term goals:** Identify long-term changes you want to implement and set timelines for achieving them.

Harmonious Home Toolkit: Practical Tools for Neurodesign-Based Living

The Harmonious Living Toolkit is designed to help you create and maintain a nurturing, balanced, and aesthetically pleasing environment in your home. Drawing on the principles of neurodesign, this toolkit includes practical tools, techniques, and resources for creating a space that promotes well-being and reflects your authentic self.

1. Mindful Space Assessment: How Your Home Affects You
Tool: Neurodesign Emotional Mapping

- **How to Use:** Walk through each room and rate your feelings on a scale of **1 (draining) to 10 (energizing)**.
- **What to Look For:** Areas that feel overwhelming, cluttered, or uncomfortable versus those that feel calming and inspiring.
- **Next Step:** Identify patterns—what elements contribute to positive emotions? What drains you? Adjust accordingly.

Tool: Sensory Audit

- **How to Use:** Assess your five senses in each space:
  - **Sight:** Is the lighting too harsh? Are colors too stimulating or dull?
  - **Sound:** Do you hear noise pollution? Can you introduce calming sounds (e.g., white noise, water features)?
  - **Touch:** Are surfaces inviting or uncomfortable? Is there enough softness and warmth?
  - **Smell:** Do scents support relaxation and focus?
  - **Taste:** Does the kitchen environment encourage mindful eating?
- **Next Step:** Adjust sensory input by changing textures, soundscapes, scents, and lighting to align with comfort and function.

2. Intentional Design Principles: Optimizing Layout and Flow
Tool: Space Functionality Scorecard

- **How to Use:** Rate each room from **1 (inefficient) to 5 (highly functional)** based on:
  - **Ease of movement** (Is the layout intuitive?)
  - **Zoning** (Does the space serve its intended purpose?)
  - **Flexibility** (Can it adapt to different needs?)

- **Next Step:** Rearrange furniture or remove unnecessary items to enhance flow.

Tool: Color Psychology Indicator

- **How to Use:** Identify the dominant colors in your home and compare them to **neuroscientific color effects:**
  - **Blues & Greens:** Calming, restorative, ideal for bedrooms and relaxation spaces.
  - **Yellows & Oranges:** Stimulating, best for kitchens and social areas.
  - **Reds:** Energizing but overwhelming in large amounts. Use in moderation.
- **Next Step:** Adjust color palettes based on how you want each space to feel.

3. Personalization Tools: Expressing Identity in Your Space
Tool: Emotional Object Inventory

- **How to Use:** Assess each item in your space with these questions:
  - Does it **bring joy,** or does it feel like clutter?
  - Is it **meaningful or functional?**
  - Does it reflect **who I am today** or an outdated version of myself?
- **Next Step:** Keep items that support your identity and remove those that don't.

Tool: Neuroaesthetic Engagement

- **How to Use:** Observe how often you engage with art and design elements in your space.
  - Do you notice your artwork, or does it fade into the background?
  - Are textures and materials pleasant to touch?

- **Next Step:** Rearrange or update décor to foster more daily engagement.

4. Comfort and Wellness Optimization
Tool: Ergonomic Comfort Assessment

- **How to Use:** Sit, stand, and move in different spaces. Rate comfort from **1 (painful) to 10 (perfect support)**.
- **Next Step:** Adjust seating, workstations, and bedding to improve posture and relaxation.

Tool: Circadian Lighting Test

- **How to Use:** Track natural light exposure in your home. Note when and where light feels too dim or too harsh.
- **Next Step:** Add warm light for evenings, cooler light for focus areas, and maximize natural light exposure during the day.

5. Nature Connection Strategies
Tool: Biophilic Design Scorecard

- **How to Use:** Score your home's connection to nature on a scale from **1 (none) to 5 (strong)**.
  - Do you have natural light access?
  - Are plants present?
  - Is there a view of nature or outdoor access?
  - Are natural materials (wood, stone) used?
- **Next Step:** Incorporate more nature-based elements to enhance biophilic benefits.

6. Maintenance and Sustainability Strategies
Tool: Decluttering Decision Matrix

- **How to Use:** For each item, ask:
  - Have I used this in the past year?

- ○ Does it serve a purpose or bring joy?
- ○ If I removed it, would I miss it?
- **Next Step:** Remove anything that fails the test to reduce stress and visual clutter.

Tool: Sustainable Home Score

- **How to Use:** Rate your home's sustainability efforts from **1 (wasteful) to 5 (eco-friendly)** based on:
  - ○ Energy-efficient lighting and appliances
  - ○ Use of sustainable materials
  - ○ Waste reduction practices
- **Next Step:** Improve sustainability by switching to eco-friendly products and reducing waste.

7. Social Connection Enhancements
Tool: Social Space Rating

- **How to Use:** Evaluate if your home supports social engagement.
  - ○ Are seating arrangements conversation-friendly?
  - ○ Are shared areas welcoming and functional?
  - ○ Is the kitchen set up to encourage gathering?
- **Next Step:** Rearrange furniture and enhance shared spaces to support connection.

Tool: Shared Space Agreements

- **How to Use:** Establish guidelines for communal areas to foster harmony in shared living.
- **Next Step:** Discuss with housemates/family to create an agreement supporting everyone's well-being.

8. Reflection and Growth Integration
Tool: Weekly Environment Check-In

- **How to Use:** Spend **5 minutes each week** reflecting on:
    - How does my space feel today?
    - What one small change can improve it?
- **Next Step:** Adjust based on insights for continuous improvement.

Tool: Future Visioning Exercise

- **How to Use:** Visualize your ideal home environment 1 year from now. What's different?
- **Next Step:** Set small, actionable goals to move toward that vision.

Conclusion
This Harmonious Living Toolkit serves as a comprehensive resource for individuals seeking to create a balanced and fulfilling home environment. By integrating these tools and principles into your life, you can create a space that not only reflects your authentic self but also enhances your overall well-being and harmony.

References

Ackerman, Joshua M., Christopher Nocera, and John A. Bargh. (2010). "Incidental Haptic Sensations Influence Social Judgments and Decisions." *Science* 328 (5986): 1712–15.

Ainsworth, Mary D. Salter. 1979. *Patterns of Attachment: A Psychological Study of the Strange Situation*. Lawrence Erlbaum Associates.

Airbib, Michael. 2021. *When Brains Meet Buildings*. Oxford University Press. https://doi.org/10.1093/med/9780190060954.001.0001.

Alkozei, Anna, Ryan Smith, Natalie Dailey, Sahi Baji, and William D. S. Killgore. 2017. "Acute Exposure to Blue Wavelength During Memory Consolidation Improves Verbal Memory Performance." *PLOS ONE* 12 (1): e0169123. https://doi.org/10.1371/journal.pone.0184884.

Altman, Irwin. (1975). *The Environment and Social Behavior: privacy, Personal Space, Territory, and Crowding*. Brooks/Cole.

Alvarsson, Jesper J., Stefan Wiens, and Mats E. Nilsson. 2010. "Stress Recovery during Exposure to Nature Sound and Environmental Noise." *International Journal of Environmental Research and Public Health* 7 (3): 1036–46.

Ando, Tadao. 2012. *Tadao Ando: Complete Works 1975–2012*. Taschen.

Appleton, Jay. 1975. *The Experience of Landscape*. John Wiley & Sons.

Aravena, Alejandro. 2016. *Elemental: Incremental Housing and Participatory Design Manual*. Hatje Cantz.

Arthur, Paul, and Romedi Passini. 1992. *Wayfinding: People, Signs, and Architecture*. McGraw-Hill.

Babisch, Wolfgang. 2014. "Updated Exposure-Response Relationship between Road Traffic Noise and Coronary Heart Diseases: A Meta-Analysis." *Noise and Health* 16 (68): 1–9.

Bachelard, Gaston. 1994. *The Poetics of Space*. Translated by Maria Jolas. Beacon Press. (Original work published 1958).

Banbury, Simon P., and D. C. Berry. 2005. "Office Noise and Employee Concentration: Identifying Causes of Disruption and Potential Improvements." *Ergonomics* 48 (1): 25–37.

Basner, Mathias, Wolfgang Babisch, Adrian Davis, et al. 2014. "Auditory and Non-Auditory Effects of Noise on Health." *The Lancet* 383 (9925): 1325–33.

Batcho, Krystine I. 2007. "Nostalgia and the Emotional Tone and Content of Song Lyrics." *American Journal of Psychology* 120 (3): 361–81.

Baumeister, Roy F., and Mark R. Leary. 1995. "The Need to Belong: Desire for Interpersonal Attachments as a Fundamental Human Motivation." *Psychological Bulletin* 117 (3): 497–529.

Berto, Rita. 2005. "Exposure to Restorative Environments and Recovery of Cognitive Functions." *Journal of Environmental Psychology* 25 (3): 249–59.

Bilbao, Tatiana. 2019. *Tatiana Bilbao Estudio: Perspectives*. Arquine.

Blesser, Barry, and Linda-Ruth Salter. 2009. *Spaces Speak, Are You Listening? Experiencing Aural Architecture*. MIT Press.

Boubekri, Mohamed, Ivy N. Cheung, Kathryn J. Reid, Chia-Hui Wang, and Phyllis C. Zee. 2014. "Impact of Windows and Daylight Exposure on Overall Health and Sleep Quality of Office Workers: A Case-Control Pilot Study." *Journal of Clinical Sleep Medicine* 10 (6): 603–11. https://doi.org/10.5664/jcsm.3780.

Bowen, Murray. 1978. *Family Therapy in Clinical Practice.* Jason Aronson.

Bowen, Murray. 2017. *Family Therapy in Clinical Practice.* Reprint ed. Jason Aronson. (Original work published 1978).

Bowlby, John. 1969. *Attachment and Loss: Volume I. Attachment.* Hogarth Press.

Bowlby, John. 1988. *A Secure Base: Parent-Child Attachment and Healthy Human Development.* Basic Books.

Boyce, Peter R. 2014. *Human Factors in Lighting.* CRC Press.

Brand, Stewart. 1994. *How Buildings Learn: What Happens After They're Built.* Viking.

Bryson, Bill. 2010. *At Home: A Short History of Private Life.* Doubleday.

Cajochen, Christian, Mirjam Münch, Szymon Kobialka, et al. 2011. "High Sensitivity of Human Melatonin, Alertness, Thermoregulation, and Heart Rate to Short Wavelength Light." *Journal of Clinical Endocrinology & Metabolism* 90 (3): 1311–16.

Carayon Pascale, Abigail R. Wooldridge, Pascale Hoonakker, Amy S. Hundt, Michelle M. Kelly. 2020. "SEIPS 3.0: Human-Centered Design of the Patient Journey for Patient Safety." *Applied Ergonomics* 84 (4): 103033. doi: 10.1016/j.apergo.2019.103033. Epub 2020 Jan 10. PMID: 31987516; PMCID: PMC7152782.

Clark, Charlotte, and David Uzzell. 2002. "The Affordances of the Home, Neighbourhood, School and Town Centre for Adolescents." *Journal of Environmental Psychology* 22 (1–2): 95–108. https://doi.org/10.1006/jevp.2001.0242.

Chatterjee, Anjan. 2013. "Neuroaesthetics: A Coming of Age Story." *Journal of Cognitive Neuroscience* 25 (3): 735–43.

Chou, Sheryl, and Michael Chou. 2023. "Sweet Smell of Success: Simple Fragrance Method Produces Major Memory Boost." *University of*

California, Irvine News. https://news.uci.edu/2023/08/01/sweet-smell-of-success-simple-fragrance-method-produces-major-memory-boost/.

Csikszentmihalyi, Mihaly, and Eugene Rochberg-Halton. 1981. *The Meaning of Things: Domestic Symbols and the Self.* Cambridge University Press.

Dijkstra, Katinka, Marcel E. Pieterse, and Adriaan Pruyn. 2008. "Stress-Reducing Effects of Indoor Plants in the Built Healthcare Environment." *The Journal of Alternative and Complementary Medicine* 14 (9): 123–29.

Dittmar, Helga. 2011. "Material Possessions as a Basis of Self-Identity or Social Status: A Biographical Analysis." *Journal of Economic Psychology* 32 (4): 579–88.

Dul, Jan, and Bernard Weerdmeester. 2008. *Ergonomics for Beginners: A Quick Reference Guide.* CRC Press.

Eagleman, David M. 2015. *The Brain: The Story of You.* Pantheon Books.

Eberhard, John Paul. 2008. *Brain Landscape: The Coexistence of Neuroscience and Architecture.* Oxford University Press.

Elliot, Andrew J., and Markus A. Maier. 2014. "Color Psychology: Effects of Perceiving Color on Psychological Functioning in Humans." *Annual Review of Psychology* 65: 95–120.

Epston, David, and David Marsten. 2016. *Narrative Therapy in Wonderland: Connecting with Children's Imaginative Know-How.* W. W. Norton & Company.

Erikson, Erik H. 1950. *Childhood and Society.* W. W. Norton & Company.

Evans, Gary W., and Richard E. Wener. 2007. "Crowding and Personal Space Invasion on the Train: Please Don't Make Me Sit in the Middle." *Journal of Environmental Psychology* 27 (1): 90–94. https://doi.org/10.1016/j.jenvp.2006.10.002.

Evans, Gary W., and Janetta M. McCoy. 1998. "When Buildings Don't Work: The Role of Architecture in Human Health." *Journal of Environmental Psychology* 18 (1): 85–94.

Ferrari, Joseph R., and Catherine A. Roster. 2018. "Delaying Disposal: Examining the Relationship Between Procrastination and Clutter Across Generations." *Current Psychology* 37 (2): 441–47.

Fivush, Robln, Jennifer G. Bohanek, and Widaad Zaman. 2011. "Personal and Intergenerational Narratives in Relation to Adolescents' Well-Being." *New Directions for Child and Adolescent Development* 2011 (131): 45–57.

Fraser, Tom, and Adam Banks. 2004. *Designer's Color Manual: The Complete Guide to Color Theory and Application*. Thames & Hudson.

Fromm, Erich. 1973. *The Anatomy of Human Destructiveness*. Holt, Rinehart & Winston.

Frost, Randy O., and Rachel C. Gross. 1993. "The Hoarding of Possessions." *Behaviour Research and Therapy* 31 (4): 367–81.

Gaggioli, Andrea. 2020. "Ergonomic Considerations in Home Office Design." *Applied Ergonomics* 82: 102956.

Gang, Jeanne. 2017. *Studio Gang: Architecture and Urbanism*. Phaidon Press.

Gehl, Jan. 2010. *Cities for People*. Island Press.

Geilman, Anna. 2016. "Designing for Children with Sensory Integration Disorders: A Handbook for Residential Designers." *JCCC Honors Journal* 8 (1): Article 3. https://scholarspace.jccc.edu/honors_journal/vol8/iss1/3.

Gifford, Robert. 2014. *Environmental Psychology: Principles and Practice*. Optimal Books.

Gillis, Kaitlyn, and Birgitta Gatersleben. 2015. "A Review of Psychological Literature on the Health and Well-Being Benefits of Biophilic Design." *Buildings* 5 (3): 948–63. https://doi.org/10.3390/buildings5030948.

Gosling, Samuel D., Robert Gifford, and Lindsay McCunn. 2013. "The Selection, Creation, and Perception of Interior Spaces: An Environmental Psychology Approach." In *The Handbook of Interior Design*, edited by Graeme Brooker and Lois Weinthal, 278–90.

Gosling, Samuel D., Sei Jin Ko, Thomas Mannarelli, and Margaret E. Morris. 2002. "A Room with a Cue: Personality Judgments Based on Offices and Bedrooms." *Journal of Personality and Social Psychology* 82 (3): 379–98.

Gottman, John M. 1999. *The Seven Principles for Making Marriage Work: A Practical Guide from the Country's Foremost Relationship Expert*. Crown Publishers.

Gottman, John M., and Julie Gottman. 2024. *The New Marriage Clinic: A Scientifically Based Marital Therapy Updated*. The Gottman Institute.

Gritzka Susan, Tadhg E. MacIntyre, Denise Dörfel, Jordan L. Baker-Blanc, and Giovanna Calogiuri. 2020. "The Effects of Workplace Nature-Based Interventions on the Mental Health and Well-Being of Employees: A Systematic Review." *Frontiers in Psychiatry* 11:323. doi: 10.3389/fpsyt.2020.00323. PMID: 32411026; PMCID: PMC7198870.

Hall, Edward T. 1966. *The Hidden Dimension*. Doubleday.

Hargreaves, David J., and Adrian C. North. 2008. *The Social and Applied Psychology of Music*. Oxford University Press. https://doi.org/10.1093/acprof:oso/9780198567424.001.0001.

Harlow, Harry F., and Stephen J. Suomi. 1970. "Nature of Love—Simplified." *American Psychologist* 25 (2): 161–68.

Hartig, Terry, Marlis Mang, and Gary W. Evans. 2003. "Restorative Effects of Natural Environment Experiences." *Journal of Environmental Psychology* 23 (2): 105–23.

Hartig, Terry, Richard Mitchell, Sjerp De Vries, and Howard Frumkin. 2014. "Nature and Health." *Annual Review of Public Health* 35: 207–28.

Harvard Medical School. 2023. "How Music Resonates in the Brain." *Harvard Medical School Magazine*.

Hendrix, Harville, and Helen LaKelly Hunt. 2008. *Getting the Love You Want: A Guide for Couples*. 20th anniversary ed. St. Martin's Griffin.

Hendrix, Harville. 2007. *Getting the Love You Want: A Guide for Couples*. 20th anniversary ed. Harry Holt & Co.

Hines, Thomas S. 2006. *Richard Neutra and the Search for Modern Architecture*. Rizzoli.

Ibrahim, Maha Mahmoud. 2019. "The Integration of Interior Design and Neuroscience: Towards a Methodology to Apply Neuroscience in Interior Spaces." *Journal of Architecture, Art & Humanistic Science* 4 (14): 36–57. https://doi.org/10.21608/mjaf.2019.25813.

Ingels, Bjarke. 2011. *Yes Is More: An Archicomic on Architectural Evolution*. Taschen.

Israel, Toby. 2003. *Some Place Like Home: Using Design Psychology to Create Ideal Places*. Wiley-Academy.

Jacobsen, Thomas. 2004. "The Early History of Research on Aesthetics and the Brain." *Brain and Cognition* 55 (2): 185–89

Jodidio, Philip. 2014. *Shigeru Ban: Complete Works 1985–2015*. Taschen.

Jonauskaite, Domicele, Ahmed Abu-Akel, Nele Dael, et al. 2020. "Universal Patterns in Color-Emotion Associations Are Further Shaped by Linguistic and Geographic Proximity." *Psychological Science* 31 (10): 1245–1260. https://doi.org/10.1177/0956797620948810.

Joye, Yannick. 2007. "Architectural Lessons from Environmental Psychology: The Case of Biophilic Architecture." *Review of General Psychology* 11 (4): 305–328. https://doi.org/10.1037/1089-2680.11.4.305.

Jung, Carl G. 1961. *Memories, Dreams, Reflections.* Translated by Richard and Clara Winston. Pantheon Books. (Original work published 1960)

Jung, Carl G. 1968. *Alchemical Studies.* Translated by R. F. C. Hull. Princeton University Press. (Original work published 1953)

Kallinen, Kari, and Niklas Ravaja. 2007. "The Psychophysiological Effects of Music on Emotions: The Role of Individual Differences." *Psychophysiology* 44 (4): 437–45. https://doi.org/10.1111/j.1469-8986.2007.00511.x.

Kamptner, Laura N. 1995. "Personal Possessions and Their Meanings in Old Age." *Ageing International* 22 (2): 21–39.

Kandel, Eric R., James H. Schwartz, and Thomas M. Jessell. 2012. *Principles of Neural Science.* 5th ed. McGraw-Hill.

Kaplan, Rachel, and Stephen Kaplan. 1989. *The Experience of Nature: A Psychological Perspective.* Cambridge University Press.

Kaplan, Stephen. 1995. "The Restorative Benefits of Nature: Toward an Integrative Framework." *Journal of Environmental Psychology* 15 (3): 169–82.

Kaya, Naz, and Margaret J. Weber. 2003. "Cross-Cultural Differences in the Perception of Crowding and Privacy Regulation: American and Turkish Students." *Journal of Environmental Psychology* 23 (3): 301–9.

Kellert, Stephen R., and Elizabeth F. Calabrese. 2015. *The Practice of Biophilic Design.* Island Press.

Keltner, Dacher, and Jonathan Haidt. 2003. "Approaching Awe, a Moral, Spiritual, and Aesthetic Emotion." *Cognition & Emotion* 17 (2): 297–314.

Koenig, Harold G. 2018. "*The Healing Power of Faith: A Scientific Basis for the Healing Power of Prayer* (2nd ed.). Templeton Press.

Kondo, Marie. 2014. *The Life-Changing Magic of Tidying Up: The Japanese Art of Decluttering and Organizing.* Ten Speed Press.

Kondo, Marie. 2016. *Spark Joy: An Illustrated Master Class on the Art of Organizing and Tidying Up*. Ten Speed Press.

Küller, Rikard, Seifeddin Ballal, Thorbjörn Laike, Byron Mikellides, and Graciela Tonello. 2009. "The Impact of Light and Colour on Psychological Mood: A Cross-Cultural Study of Indoor Work Environments." *Ergonomics* 49 (14): 1496–1507. https://doi.org/10.1080/00140130600858142.

Kuo, Frances E. 2015. "How Might Contact with Nature Promote Human Health?" *Acta Psychologica Sinica* 47 (3): 146–54.

Labbé, Daniel, Natalie Schmidt, and Jean Babin. 2007. "The Effect of Soft Music on the Levels of Anxiety and Stress in a Clinical Setting." *Journal of Music Therapy* 44 (2): 105–18. https://doi.org/10.1093/jmt/44.2.105.

Lane, Andrew M., Peter C. Terry, and Lorraine Keohane. 1998. "The Influence of Mood on Performance in Sports: A Meta-Analysis of the Profile of Mood States (POMS) and Its Uses in Sports Psychology." *Journal of Sports Sciences* 16 (5): 469–78. https://doi.org/10.1080/026404198366240.

Le Corbusier. 1931. *Vers une Architecture* [Towards an Architecture]. The Architectural Press.

Le Corbusier. 1986. *Towards a New Architecture*. Translated by Frederick Etchells. Dover Publications. (Original work published 1931)

Leder, Helmut, Benno Belke, Andries Oeberst, and Dorothee Augustin. 2014. "A Model of Aesthetic Appreciation and Aesthetic Judgments." *British Journal of Psychology* 95 (4): 489–508.

Levine, Peter A., and Ann Frederick. 1997. *Waking the Tiger: Healing Trauma: The Innate Capacity to Transform Overwhelming Experiences*. North Atlantic Books.

Lidwell, William, Kritina Holden, and Jill Butler. 2010. *Universal Principles of Design, Revised and Updated: 125 Ways to Enhance Usability, Influence Perception, Increase Appeal, Make Better Design Decisions, and Teach Through Design*. Rockport Publishers.

Loewy, Joanne. 2020. "Music Therapy for Stress Reduction." *International Journal of Music Therapy* 25 (2): 201–16.

Mallett, Shelley. 2004. "Understanding Home: A Critical Review of the Literature." *Sociological Review* 52: 62–89.

Marcus, Clare Cooper. 2006. *House as a Mirror of Self: Exploring the Deeper Meaning of Home*. Nicolas-Hays.

Marquardt, Gesine, and Peter Schmieg. 2009. "Dementia-Friendly Architecture: Environments That Facilitate Wayfinding in Nursing Homes." *American Journal of Alzheimer's Disease & Other Dementias* 24 (4): 333–40.

Maslow, Abraham H. 1943. "A Theory of Human Motivation." *Psychological Review* 50 (4): 370–96. https://doi.org/10.1037/h0054346.

Maslow, Abraham H. 1970. *Motivation and Personality*. Harper & Row.

Maxwell, Joseph A. 2006. *Qualitative Research Design: An Interactive Approach* (2nd ed.). Sage Publications.

McCarter, Robert. 2006. *Frank Lloyd Wright*. Phaidon Press.

McMains, Stephanie, and Sabine Kastner. 2011. "Interactions of Top-Down and Bottom-Up Mechanisms in Human Visual Cortex." *Journal of Neuroscience* 31 (2): 587–97. https://doi.org/10.1523/JNEUROSCI.3766-10.2011.

Mehta, Ravi, and Rui (Juliet) Zhu. 2009. "Blue or Red? Exploring the Effect of Color on Cognitive Task Performances." *Science* 323 (5918): 1226–29. https://doi.org/10.1126/science.1169144.

Merriam-Webster. n.d.a. "Ergonomics." In *Merriam-Webster.com Dictionary*. Retrieved February 5, 2023, from https://www.merriam-webster.com/dictionary/ergonomics.

Merriam-Webster. n.d.b. "Proxemics." In *Merriam-Webster.com Dictionary*. Retrieved February 5, 2023, from https://www.merriam-webster.com/dictionary/proxemics.

Minuchin, Salvador, Michael D. Reiter, and Charmaine Borda. 2021. *The Craft of Family Therapy: Challenging Certainties*. 2nd ed. Routledge.

Mitchell, Lynne, and Elizabeth Burton. 2006. "Neighbourhoods for Life: Designing Dementia-Friendly Outdoor Environments." *Quality in Ageing and Older Adults* 7 (1): 26–33.

Munzel, Thomas, Frank P. Schmidt, Sebastian Steven, Johanne Horzog, Andreas Daiber, and Mette Sorensen. 2018. "Environmental Noise and the Cardiovascular System: The Epidemiological and Mechanistic Evidence of the Impacts of Noise on Human Health." *International Journal of Environmental Research and Public Health* 15 (8): 1428. https://doi.org/10.3390/ijerph15081428.

Murphy, Michael, and Jeffrey Mansfield. 2020. *The Architecture of Health: Hospital Design and the Construction of Dignity*. Cooper Hewitt, Smithsonian Design Museum.

Murphy, Michael. 2020. "Health-Focused Architecture: A Focus on the Butaro District Hospital in Rwanda." MASS Design Group.

Murthy, Vivek H. 2015. *Step It Up! The Surgeon General's Call to Action to Promote Walking and Walkable Communities*. U.S. Department of Health and Human Services.

Neave, Nick, Sarah Wolfson, and Rebecca Ackerley. 2017. "Messy Bedrooms and Untidy Offices: Clutter and Well-Being." *Personality and Individual Differences* 104: 441–45.

Nieuwenhuis, Marlon, Craig Knight, Tom Postmes, and S. Alexander Haslam. 2014. "The Relative Benefits of Green versus Lean Office Space: Three Field Experiments." *Journal of Experimental Psychology: Applied* 20 (3): 199–214. https://doi.org/10.1037/xap0000024.

Parcells, Claudia, Manfred Stommel, and Robert P. Hubbard. 2010. "Mismatch of Classroom Furniture and Student Body Dimensions: Empirical

Findings and Health Implications." *Journal of Adolescent Health* 24 (4): 265–73.

Passini, Romedi, Constant Rainville, Nicolas Marchand, and Yves Joanette. 2000. "Wayfinding in Dementia: Some Research Findings and a New Look at Design." *Journal of Architectural and Planning Research* 17 (2): 133–51.

Peretz, Isabelle, and Robert Zatorre. 2005. "Brain Organization for Music Processing." *Annual Review of Psychology* 56: 89–114. https://doi.org/10.1146/annurev.psych.56.091103.070225.

Pheasant, Stephen, and Christine M. Haslegrave. 2006. *Bodyspace: Anthropometry, Ergonomics, and the Design of Work*. CRC Press.

Riva, Giuseppe. 2018. "The Neuroscience of Body Memory: From the Self through the Space to the Others." *Cortex* 104: 241–60. https://doi.org/10.1016/j.cortex.2017.07.013.

Rogers, Carl R. 1980. *A Way of Being*. Houghton Mifflin.

Rogers, Carl R., and Harold Lyon. 2013. *On Becoming an Effective Teacher: Person-Centered Teaching, Psychology, Philosophy, and Dialogues with Carl R. Rogers and Harold Lyon*. Routledge.

Rogers, Kara. 2019. "Biophilia Hypothesis." *Encyclopedia Britannica*. June 25. https://www.britannica.com/science/biophilia-hypothesis.

Ronnberg, Ami, and Kathleen Martin, eds. 2010. *The Book of Symbols: Reflections on Archetypal Images*. Taschen.

Rubinstein, Robert I., and Patricia A. Parmelee. 1992. "Attachment to Place and the Representation of the Life Course by the Elderly." *Place Attachment* 137 (3): 139–63.

Saarikallio, Suvi. 2011. "Music as Emotional Self-Regulation throughout Adulthood." *Psychology of Music* 39 (3): 307–27.

Saxbe, Darby E., and Rena L. Repetti. 2010. "No Place Like Home: Home Tours Correlate with Daily Patterns of Mood and Cortisol."

Personality and Social Psychology Bulletin 36 (1): 71–81. https://doi.org/10.1177/0146167209352864.

Sedikides, Constantine, Tim Wildschut, Jamie Arndt, and Clay Routledge. 2008. "Nostalgia: Past, Present, and Future." *Current Directions in Psychological Science* 17 (5): 304–7.

Seligman, Martin E. 2011. *Flourish: A Visionary New Understanding of Happiness and Well-Being.* Free Press.

Seligman, Martin E. 2012. *Flourish: A Visionary New Understanding of Happiness and Well-Being.* Atria Paperback.

Silvia, Paul J., and Elizabeth M. Brown. 2007. "Anger, Disgust, and the Negative Aesthetic Emotions: Expanding an Appraisal Model of Aesthetic Experience." *Psychology of Aesthetics, Creativity, and the Arts* 1 (2): 100–106.

Sixsmith, Andrew, and Judith Sixsmith. 2008. "Ageing in Place in the United Kingdom." *Ageing International* 32 (3): 219–35.

Smith, Jeffrey K. 2014. "The Psychology of Aesthetics and the Arts." In *Oxford Handbook of Cognitive Psychology.*

Smith, Susan G. 1994. "The Essential Qualities of a Home." *Journal of Environmental Psychology* 14: 21–30. https://doi.org/10.1016/S0272-4944(05)80196-3.

Söderlund, Jana, and Peter Newman. 2017. "Biophilic Architecture: A Review of the Rationale and Outcomes." *Buildings* 7 (4): 15–29

Sommer, Robert, and Hugh Ross. 1958. "Social Interaction on a Geriatrics Ward." *International Journal of Social Psychiatry* 4 (2): 128–33. https://doi.org/10.1177/002076405800400207.

Sommer, Robert, and Humphry Osmond. 1960. "Autobiographies of Former Mental Patients." *Journal of Mental Science* 106 (443): 648–62. https://doi.org/10.1192/bjp.106.443.648.

Sommer, Robert. 1969. *Personal Space: The Behavioral Basis of Design.* Prentice-Hall.

Stanczyk Malgorzata M. 2011. "Music Therapy in Supportive Cancer Care." *Reports of Practical Oncology & Radiotherapy* 16 (5):170–72. doi: 10.1016/j.rpor.2011.04.005. PMID: 24376975; PMCID: PMC3863265.

Steele, Fritz. 1980. *The Sense of Place.* CBI Publishing Company.

Stokols, Daniel. 1972. "On the Distinction Between Density and Crowding: Some Implications for Future Research." *Psychological Review* 79 (3): 275–77. https://doi.org/10.1037/h0032975.

Sullivan, William C., and Frances E. Kuo. 2007. "The Greening of Urban Spaces: Evidence from Crime and Social Capital Research." *Environment and Behavior* 39 (5): 679–705.

Sundstrom, Eric, Paul A. Bell, Paul L. Busby, and Cheryl Asmus. 1996. "Environmental Psychology 1989–1994." *Annual Review of Psychology* 47: 485–512. https://doi.org/10.1146/annurev.psych.47.1.485.

Tajfel, Henri, and John C. Turner. 1979. "An Integrative Theory of Intergroup Conflict." In *The Social Psychology of Intergroup Relations*, William G. Austin and Stephen Worchel, eds. 33–47. Brooks/Cole.

Tatkin, Stan. 2011. *Wired for Love: How Understanding Your Partner's Brain and Attachment Style Can Help You Defuse Conflict and Build a Secure Relationship.* New Harbinger Publications.

Taylor, Richard P., Branka Spehar, Peter Van Donkelaar, and Caroline M. Hagerhall. 2011. "Perceptual and Physiological Responses to Jackson Pollock's Fractals." *Frontiers in Human Neuroscience* 5: 60.

Tomassoni, Rosella, Giuseppe Galetta, and Eugenia Treglia. 2015. "Psychology of Light: How Light Influences the Health and Psyche." *Psychology* 6: 1216–22. https://doi.org/10.4236/psych.2015.610119.

Ulrich, Roger S. 1984. "View Through a Window May Influence Recovery from Surgery." *Science* 224 (4647): 420–21. https://doi.org/10.1126/science.6143402.

Ulrich, Roger S., Robert F. Simons, Barbara D. Losito, Evelyn Fiorito, Mark A. Miles, and Michael Zelson. 1991. "Stress Recovery During Exposure to Natural and Urban Environments." *Journal of Environmental Psychology* 11 (3): 201–30.

U.S. Department of Health and Human Services. 2023. *Our Epidemic of Loneliness and Isolation: The U.S. Surgeon General's Advisory on the Healing Effects of Social Connection and Community*. U.S. Public Health Service. https://www.hhs.gov/sites/default/files/surgeon-general-social-connection-advisory.pdf.

van den Berg, Agnes E., Sander L. Koole, and Nickie Y. van der Wulp. 2003. "Environmental Preferences and Restoration." *Journal of Environmental Psychology* 23 (2): 135–46. https://doi.org/10.1016/S0272-4944(02)00111-7.

Veitch, Jennifer A., and Anca D. Galasiu. 2012. "The Physiological and Psychological Effects of Windows, Daylight, and View at Home: Review of the Evidence." *Journal of Environmental Psychology* 32 (4): 314–23.

Vischer, Jacqueline C. 2008. "Towards an Environmental Psychology of Workspace: How People Are Affected by Environments for Work." *Architectural Science Review* 51 (2): 97–108.

Vohs, Kathleen D., Joseph P. Redden, and Ryan Rahinel. 2013. "Physical Order Produces Healthy Choices, Generosity, and Conventionality, Whereas Disorder Produces Creativity." *Psychological Science* 24 (9): 1860–67.

Weisman, Jerry. 1981. "Evaluating Architectural Legibility: Way-Finding in the Built Environment." *Environment and Behavior* 13 (2): 189–204.

Yin, Jie, Shihao Zhu, Piers MacNaughton, Joseph G. Allen, and John D. Spengler. 2018. "Physiological and Cognitive Performance of Exposure to Biophilic Indoor Environment." *Building and Environment* 132: 148–56. https://doi.org/10.1016/j.buildenv.2018.01.006.

Zeki, Semir. 1999. "Art and the Brain." *Scientific American* 280 (4): 70–77.

Zumthor, Peter. 1999. *Thinking Architecture*. Birkhäuser.

About the Author

Rachel Melvald, also known as the psychitect, is an Ohioan transplant to California. Often referred to as "the Marie Kondo of the West," she is a licensed psychotherapist with a background in fine arts, architecture, and psychology. She specializes in helping her clients maintain good relationships—both romantic and professional—during the design process while also curating environments that promote healing and reflect their basic psychological needs and higher well-being.

Notes

www.ingramcontent.com/pod-product-compliance
Lightning Source LLC
Chambersburg PA
CBHW071701090426
42738CB00009B/1622